WORKING MEN'S COLLEGE.

LIBRARY REGULATIONS.

The Library is open every week-day evening, from 6.30 to 10 o'clock, except on Saturdays, when it closes at 9.

This book may be kept for three weeks. If not returned within that period, the borrower will be liable to a fine of one penny per week.

If lost or damaged, the borrower will be required to make good such loss or damage.

Only one book may be borrowed at a time.

THE APPROACH TO TEACHING

THE
APPROACH
TO TEACHING

By

HERBERT WARD, C.B.E., M.A.

LATE CHIEF INSPECTOR FOR THE TRAINING OF
TEACHERS, AND FORMERLY HOUSE TUTOR
BOROUGH ROAD TRAINING COLLEGE

and

FRANK ROSCOE, M.A.

SECRETARY THE TEACHERS REGISTRATION COUNCIL
AND SOMETIME LECTURER IN EDUCATION IN
THE UNIVERSITY OF BIRMINGHAM

LONDON
G. BELL & SONS, LTD.
1928

PRINTED IN GREAT BRITAIN BY PURNELL AND SONS
PAULTON (SOMERSET) AND LONDON

CONTENTS

THE
APPROACH TO TEACHING

CHAPTER I

INTRODUCTORY

THIS book, as its title shows, is intended for the young teacher, the beginner. It is not written to replace the longer and fuller treatises and manuals of teaching : it is to serve rather as an introduction to them. Accordingly it makes no attempt to survey, in an orderly way, the theoretical basis of teaching, or, except very partially, to discuss the relation of teaching to education as a whole. Nor does it examine in great detail rival methods of teaching, or aim at supplying the reader with complete particulars of the methods that are commended. The principle running through the book is that the teacher makes his own method. He cannot do so without advice, unless he is one of those rare geniuses who are independent of all suggestion, and who never imitate. Advice and not prescription is the purpose of the following chapters.

In the considered opinion of the writers, the young teacher should concentrate his attention upon acquiring craftsmanship in teaching. Craftsmanship implies a great deal more than technique, though technique is naturally an important element in it. A true craftsman knows his material and has the " feel " of it, a sense of what can be made of it. He knows his tools and handles them with skill and with economy of effort. Moreover he has before his eyes the result he is aiming at, the completed artistic product, and in essence this means the possession of an ideal.

Even if the analogy of teaching with craft cannot be pressed too far, it is sufficiently close to warrant a comparison. The craftsman can learn only by doing, and the teacher learn to teach by teaching. Both must give their best endeavours to avoiding gross blunders, to learning from inevitable slips and mistakes, to a steady examination of their experience in order to improve. Both must be ready to listen to what fellow craftsmen have to advise, and to profit by what they see, hear and read. In all their striving for perfection, both must cherish an ideal. There is no inconsistency, therefore, when a teacher tries to attain craftsmanship, and at the same time preserves a sense of his high calling.

In order to become a good teaching craftsman, the beginner will have to be alive to the existence of practical problems, which it is the business of this book to indicate. They will arise in the management of boys and girls as individuals and in classes, in the choice of what he is to teach, and how he is to teach it, even in the disposition and use of his classroom and the furniture and materials in it.

But troublesome as these problems are bound to be, the beginner will be wise to spare time also for some reflection upon the meaning and purpose of the profession he has chosen. He may usefully ask himself : Why do we teach ? Why do we teach in schools ? Why is there a special profession of teaching ? The thoughtful person will find no difficulty in discovering at least a provisional answer to these questions. Other questions are not so easy to answer. What exactly *is* teaching ? Is it the same thing as instruction ? Is education co-extensive with teaching ? Is all teaching, and still more, is all education, confined to schools, that is, to organisations specially set apart for the purpose ? Obviously not, but then, if not, what is school teaching and what school education ? What are their aims and purposes ?

Without going fully into the theory of education, it is appropriate here to mention some of the answers that have been given. For instance, Professor Campagnac, in a recent book, thus defines the aims of education. " Children are to be made fit to live, and also fit to live with." These simple terms, if closely examined, go a long way. " Fit to live," among other things, means that the child should possess knowledge which will enable him to support himself and conduct himself as a citizen of a civilised state, and should be trained to use the knowledge that he has. " Fit to live with " means that he must be able and willing to serve the community of which he is a member.

Both imply a great deal more than positive knowledge ; they imply readiness to learn, interest in learning, willingness to work and take trouble, perseverance ; and with these personal virtues, the social virtues also, honest and just dealing, kindliness in intercourse, politeness, chivalry, loyal co-operation with one's fellows, and subordination to the needs of the community—in short, character. This conception perhaps overstresses the weight of society. But it is not inconsistent with Professor Campagnac's view to suggest, as other writers do, that education may also be considered as the expansion and realisation of the latent powers of the pupil, as the due satisfaction of his natural and legitimate instincts and interests, as well as the development of any special abilities he may have. As another writer, Professor Bompas Smith, puts it, education is to make the pupils live " more valuable lives," valuable to themselves and to the society in which they find themselves.

This brief sketch of the ultimate problems will serve perhaps to start the reflective beginner upon his meditations. He may ask himself further, how far the qualities that are desired are and can be cultivated at home, before or during the school period, what the school has to contribute, what particular contributions are given by schools of different kinds, what advantages a large school has over a smaller, and on the other hand what advantages has a small school, for example, a small private school, over a larger. The young teacher may also with benefit to himself reflect upon the place of his own school in the community, and how it subserves the general ends of society.

The purport of what has been just said is to suggest that the young teacher should, in a tentative way, construct his own working philosophy of education, to serve him until his experience and his reading enable him, if he is so disposed, to formulate for himself a more systematic theory. We think he will be well advised to limit himself to inquiries and reflections of the kind just touched upon at any rate during the early years when he is mastering his craft. For he must concentrate upon this first. It is not an affair of following a well-remembered routine, though imitation of his own former teachers has its value. Still less is it the application of tips and dodges, though such practical hints are not to be disdained. In order to teach well the teacher must be master of his own knowledge and master of his class. Only so far as he controls both efficiently can he hope to teach, to bring the necessary knowledge to bear on the pupils, and induce in them the right attitude towards the things they have to learn.

Something will be said in later chapters on all three aspects of the art of teaching. To adapt a phrase of Sir John Adams, if the teacher's business is to teach John arithmetic he must know both arithmetic and John. To teach well he must learn to bring arithmetic and John together. Whether, in teaching John arithmetic, the teacher can also train and educate him in a higher sense than that of mere instruction will also have to be considered. But for the beginner skill in instruction is, in the view of the present writers, of paramount importance. We hope to demonstrate that the craft of teaching, if it is really workmanlike, travels a long way towards the higher ends of real education. It is not limited, as it seems to be, to instruction.

Problems of the curriculum will not be here discussed. The young teacher, happily for him, is not called upon to decide what he is to teach his charges. In the schools where they find themselves the beginners have their subjects already prescribed ; and very commonly have set before them the precise amount they are expected to accomplish in a term or in a year. The subjects we shall discuss are the common subjects ordinarily taught in schools. They will be treated as separate subjects, and questions such as whether it is possible to amalgamate some of them, or if it is right to bring those which are regarded as humbler subjects into a position of greater prominence will be designedly avoided. Experiments are being carried on not only in connection with curriculum but more generally in connection with methods which may ultimately affect teaching in all schools. The young teacher should be ready to be interested in them. But, until he is well on his feet, he had better content himself with following the best current general practice and try to make himself perfect in it.

This pursuit of good craftsmanship is worth while, not only because it improves the efficiency of the teacher, but also because it gives interest to the work, tempering the dullness of inevitable routine with a spirit of adventure. The subject matter set forth in the syllabus may be elementary, and its repetition tedious ; the school conditions and procedure may often appear irksome, but for the alert-minded teacher there is always compensation in the infinite diversity of youthful minds, and in the quest of a technical skill which is at once flexible and adequate.

CHAPTER II

THE YOUNG TEACHER

OUR laws demand that all children between the ages of five and fourteen shall be under efficient instruction. Outside these ages there are, of course, very many who seek instruction. It follows that the work of teaching engages the services of probably not less than 200,000 men and women, while the annual recruiting runs to nearly 10,000. These large totals should serve to remind the beginner that teaching is a form of work in which, as in other professions, there are many who cannot claim to possess special endowments or native genius. He should remember that he is joining a body which undertakes a national work, and which is composed, of necessity and in the main, of those who can satisfy the requirements of good craftsmanship without rising to the level of such distinguished performance as will transcend all technical rules. In practice the work may be undertaken by any well-balanced and healthy young man or woman who has the requisite educational equipment, and is ready and willing to learn the craft of teaching.

There are, no doubt, very many " born " teachers, with a natural knack of managing children, and with natural powers of teaching. Many a parent, especially many a mother, and many elder brothers and sisters, educated and uneducated alike, exercise their natural gifts without being aware that they possess them. But the greater number of those who actually teach in schools have to acquire the art, sometimes easily, sometimes with labour. Children, up to the number of six millions, are daily under instruction, on good lines or on poor lines, and the huge organisation does not break down in practice. Weaknesses there are in plenty, no doubt, and pessimists tell us that the results are poor, but if we take into account the whole work of the schools it cannot be affirmed that they fail. Be that as it may, the point here emphasised is that the teaching profession is made up, for the most part, of ordinary, well-disposed, reasonably qualified, reasonably successful people, and that no one who is inclined to join it need be deterred by the feeling that the work of teaching is beyond his powers.

Some beginners fall into the opposite extreme and are " cocksure." Those who display this excess of self-confidence are commonly persons who have had least experience, and have given least thought to what they are about. Courage and a firm belief in one's ability to succeed are not inconsistent with a proper modesty, but " cocksureness " in one who is, after all, a tyro is wholly out of place.

Whether he is diffident or self-confident, the budding teacher cannot escape the duty of taking pains to acquire craftsmanship. Even the " born teacher " requires training and experience before he can employ his native powers with effect.

Training also, whether undertaken formally in a Training College, or less formally in the school of experience, should imply a deliberate intention and a set purpose on the part of the person under training, to perfect himself in his art. The teacher must, in a very real sense, train himself. This and the following chapters are written for his help and encouragement.

It is assumed that the beginner has actual knowledge of what he is to teach his class. He has passed examinations after a school course which is planned to give him at least a general education. One of the first things he must learn is that the knowledge which is freshest to him may be of little use to his class. It will have to be reviewed and often re-cast before he can present it to his pupils. Eager young teachers, full of the matter of their recent studies, are prone to unload their stores upon their unfortunate classes. In English they may dwell on the glories of the Romantic Revival, or, in history, upon fascinating generalisations about the Industrial Revolution to a class which can barely appreciate a simple poem of Wordsworth or which has no clear idea of the meaning either of industry or of revolution. In mathematics and science, they are apt to take for granted that the class knows the elements as thoroughly as they do themselves.

This kind of error with a teacher of common sense cures itself in time. The blank looks of the

class will soon inform a master that the excellent
stuff he is offering is above their heads. He will
just have to try and try until he has found what
does go home. But it will save much time and
disappointment if the beginner, at the outset, will
give thought to this principle, and in preparing his
lessons, will examine his material, as well as he
can, from the point of view of his pupils. He must,
of course, beware of falling into the other extreme,
that of underestimating the capacity of the class.
But the temptation to overestimate it is more likely
to befall him.

The young teacher may find himself called upon
to teach subjects of which he feels that he knows
very little. The science man may be asked to
teach grammar or literature and the arts man
elementary mathematics or easy science. This will
usually occur only in classes of children under 11
or at any rate under 14. What is he to do? In
the first place certainly not to cry off on the plea
that he is a specialist, and knows only a limited
range of subjects. Specialisation has not gone so
far that schools with children of the ages named
can be taught exclusively by specialist teachers. In
most schools, with younger classes, there are form
subjects to be taken by the form-master or mistress.

If the young teacher finds himself in the quandary
described, there is nothing for him but to learn
the new subject or—as will usually be the case—to
furbish up his old knowledge. It will do him good
to become once more a boy of 8 or 11, casting his
mind back to his own knowledge and interests at

that period. If his education has been worth anything he can rapidly learn the elements of a new subject, so closely allied, as it will ordinarily be, to those with which he is familiar. From some points of view no doubt he will teach the strange subject less well ; from others he will teach better because he will be laying his mind alongside that of his class and learning with them, a salutary process for both, if it is not carried too far. Perhaps drawing and music may be regarded as exceptions to what has been said just now. But even here, few are so ill-equipped that they cannot learn enough to carry on with a class in the hope that as the pupils pass up the school they will come under a more skilled practitioner. Unfortunate as it is, the contingency does arise, and must be faced by the young teacher.

All this suggests an attitude of mind which is essential to success in teaching. A teacher must be willing to learn from his class, be sensitive, observant, ready to take hints from his experience; patient and tolerant with youthful perverseness. Any person who is always irritated by the slow progress of his pupils, always impatient at their " stupidity," and without a fellow feeling for them, had better never try to teach. He will certainly be too blind to perceive his own faults, and will probably be too opinionated to change his methods.

These commonplaces need not be laboured. It is obvious that a good teacher must want to teach and like to teach. He should also be ready to train himself. In studying how to do so, however, he need not be either sentimental or introspectively morbid. Steady patience and tolerance do not mean a flabby acquiescence in whatever children do ; still less do they involve a sloppy emotionalism which gushes over the quaint phenomena of childhood, and never recognises the hard facts that children have to learn, and that they are not always eager or quick to learn. Nor, when the beginner is trying to train himself in his craft, should he worry over his soul, as it were, and examine his conscience too frequently.

There are two safeguards to be suggested. One is that the young teacher should preserve a sense of humour. This, of course, does not mean that he is to aim at facetiousness in class. To be under a teacher who is always " funny " is a dreary experience, as annoying to children as the family friend who is always teasing. For children like to be taken seriously. Occasions enough will occur where fun is in place : but fun is a very different thing from facetiousness.

The teacher's sense of humour should make him mock at himself from time to time, and smile at his own efforts. When he pictures himself, an average individual, very young, one lately seated on a school bench with boys such as he has before him, now attempting the delicate task of guiding the development of the intelligence and the character of his pupils, he should gently chuckle at the incongruity and at his own presumption. Viewed in some lights the task is one for a transcendent personality. But it has to be done by workaday men and women.

So when he is laying down the law from his desk
and his obedient scholars are listening with all
their ears, and accepting as incontrovertible truth
what he says, he may quietly realise the element
of absurdity in the situation. Again, if he can regard
his boys neither as monsters of iniquity nor as
wingless angels, but as comical little creatures whose
oddities one can endure, it will help to season an
existence which at times does require some relief.
A real sense of humour will effectively check any
tendency to priggishness and professional solemnity.
Those who possess the sense are, because of it and
not in spite of it, teachers of real seriousness backed
by deep-seated enthusiasm.

The second safeguard against a worrying over-
conscientiousness is that the young teacher should
learn to criticise himself in a detached way. Many
young teachers have almost tortured themselves in
the past over their mistakes because they were
taught to look upon a temporary failure in teaching
as if it were a mortal sin. Let them regard themselves as learning a difficult craft, at the beginning
of which they are bound to blunder and make
mistakes. They should, like a craftsman in wood,
sincerely regret their failures, but like the true
craftsman they should examine the causes and
learn by their errors. They need not be plunged
into despair, any more than they would be if they
were to play a false note or two in their early lessons
on the violin.

This applies to method and to discipline alike.
When the teacher can say candidly to himself or

to another : " That was a bad lesson ; I talked too much and went too fast," or " I did the wrong thing to quell young Jones,"—he is on the way to become a sound critic and a good teacher. But he need not spend a sleepless night on this account. Self-criticism of the kind suggested is a sign of self-respect, not of self-depreciation.

All this is not to condone the serious shortcomings to which the human nature of teachers, as of other people, is liable. No one can make light of slackness, of insincerity, or slovenliness, of failure to persevere, or want of conscientiousness. If the teacher, young or old, is convinced of sin under any of these heads, he should repent in the secrecy of his own chamber. But mistakes in craftsmanship due to want of experience and skill, when they are perceived, should be candidly criticised by the culprit himself, in order that they may be avoided in future.

It is not necessary to speak at length on the personal qualities desirable in a teacher. Without seeking to be a paragon, he should have patience and good temper, a ready sympathy with children, some humility and also a proper pride. He will neither bully nor cajole. With experience, but hardly without it, he will know when to be firm and when to be lenient. The young teacher, fresh from his student days, is apt to think too lightly of the importance of bearing, dress and language. He will have to remind himself that as a teacher he is under a kind of scrutiny to which he has not been submitted for some time. He cannot yet afford to be eccentric in manner or in dress. So slovenliness and lounging and off-hand attitudes generally are to be avoided.

The right use of language is in reality a point of technique, and deserves careful consideration. There are people who naturally possess pleasing voices, with clear utterance delivered without effort and heard with ease. Most teachers, however, have definitely to set themselves to the business of speaking to a class. The young teacher will have to find for himself the pitch at which his voice carries best, and this pitch must be practised until it can be maintained easily and naturally and without any forcing. Women, in particular, may permanently harm their voices by wrong use. The speech need not be, and should not be, loud in a bad sense : a class soon becomes used to quiet tones which are clear and unmistakable.

Teachers are apt to forget that a loud voice, which can hardly fail at the same time to be hard, and is often monotonous, has an intangible but real result in irritating those who listen to it for long. A teacher is often at cross-purposes with his class merely because the quality of his voice ruffles the nerves of his hearers and his own. It suggests a desire to hector and bully when the speaker means only to be business-like. No elaborate " voice production " is necessary ; an educated person usually has a mode of speaking which is natural and adequate for the purpose of teaching ; he must not force his voice. He is holding conversation with his class, under special conditions, it is true, but the voice and demeanour of conversation should be maintained.

Above all, speech must not be too rapid. There are at least two kinds of disagreeably rapid speech : one is where the speaker races through a sentence or long phrase, the other where he races through a single word of many syllables, or short phrase. Some bad speakers do both : the best public speakers do neither, and the teacher is, after all, a public speaker to his class. Distinct articulation, not an articulation blurred by a careless sliding, is of course essential. For the sake of clearness even a little exaggeration in precision is pardonable ; but the speaker must stop short of complete artificiality. The question of speech will come up again in a later chapter, when it will be appropriate to discuss the quality of the language a teacher should employ.

More need not be said on the teacher as a person. We regard him not as an Admirable Crichton or as a missionary, but as an average person, with a desire to earn his living in the honourable profession of teaching, and to do his best for those who come under his care. He is not a complete novice, because, consciously or not, he must have tried to teach someone ; at any rate he knows what he has to teach, and he has seen boys and girls before. But he has to learn the craftsmanship of his profession, and get over his awkwardness as speedily and as intelligently as possible. He should strive to attain " style " in teaching no less sedulously than the young cricketer strives for " style " in batting or in bowling.

B

CHAPTER III

THE PUPIL

THIS book is concerned with the teaching of children, and with the principles by which the teacher should be guided in teaching children, usually in schools. Some of these principles can be equally well applied to any kind of teaching, from the pulpit or platform as well as from the teacher's desk, in Universities and classes for adults as well as in the ordinary school or in the family circle. One such principle is that the teacher, in school or out of it, should know something of the persons he is trying to instruct. No more fruitful cause of want of success at home, in the classroom, or in the pulpit can be found than a failure to realise the nature and characteristics of the audience. Hence it has been often asserted that all teachers should be acquainted with psychology, the science of the mind, and especially with the psychology of children. " Child-Study " has been advocated as an essential preliminary to teaching.

It may be allowed that no systematic theory of education could be constructed without psychology. But this science, which in itself is not concerned

with education at all, is very far from easy to
beginners. It introduces them into a region of
thought and investigation which is unlike anything
they have studied before. Before any practical
application is reached, the student must cover a
great deal of ground, learn a new vocabulary,
which is all the more perplexing because some
elements in it have a dangerously familiar meaning,
and approach the very greatest of problems, such
as the inter-relation of mind and body, which
engage the attention of the profoundest thinkers.

Psychology is no longer the comparatively easy
descriptive science which it appeared to be fifty
years ago ; it is full of unsolved questions, and of
terms to which psychologists attach different meanings ; and it demands a maturity of experience
and a capacity for moving easily in the region of
the abstract which are not to be expected in a
young teacher. It is true that very many teachers,
young as well as older, are fascinated and rightly
fascinated by it, finding that it illuminates their
experience in schools, and even contributes to the
solution of their difficulties. Such teachers are not,
of course, to be discouraged from pursuing their
bent ; and many others, rebuffed at first by the
apparent dryness and remoteness of the science,
may yield to its attractions later on, when they
feel the need for a systematic co-ordination of their
observations and experience. But the beginner
should not think himself obliged to study formal
psychology, as a condition of taking his work in
a serious spirit,

Yet, without embarking upon a voyage he dreads, he ought to feel bound to learn something about his pupils. The teacher is to teach arithmetic to John: he should know arithmetic, and he should know John. In the great triangular enterprise, with teacher, John, and arithmetic all taking part in what is so often a conflict, when it might be a co-operation, John must not be taken for granted. The thoughtful teacher will wish to know how his pupils look at the world, what they like to do and enjoy doing, what they rebel against, how their immature minds work, how they learn and why they forget, what attracts their interest and holds their attention, why interest fades and attention ceases, how they can be stimulated, persuaded, induced and even, where necessary, compelled to learn. How is he to do it?

In the first place let him remember that he is a psychologist in the making already : if he is not, he should give up the attempt to teach. His own childhood is not far distant, and he can recall his own feelings, actions and ambitions ; he can reflect upon his former companions and their characteristics, upon his own reactions to school, what lessons he liked and why, what he detested and why. He can assume both that he and his acquaintances are normal, and that his pupils are normal, until he is convinced to the contrary, and that all the strange differences in thoughts and ambitions encountered or observed, are only the complex variations of the normal human being.

Besides specific experiences of his own which resemble those of his pupils, he has had other sorts of experience in his family and his social circle, all of which will contribute to his stock of psychological knowledge. He may have been fortunate enough to know intimately children younger than himself, when he was already of an age to observe them. Moreover, as an educated person, he is already familiar with the psychological terms that form an important element in our normal vocabulary. Without perhaps being able accurately to define them, he understands sensation, thought, intelligence, memory, imagination, observation, attention, habit, instinct, feeling, emotion, motive, purpose, will, character. The surface and popular meaning of these terms may be accepted as a start, and they may form a basis for the observation of his pupils that the young teacher is urged always to undertake.

Thus the beginner is possessed already of a good deal of knowledge about his pupils, if he will use it ; knowledge, it is true, unsystematic and in a sense haphazard, but not valueless. It will enable the teacher to put himself in the place of his pupils, and a little observation and the employment of his own natural wits will enable him to understand and interpret the behaviour of the pupils in his charge. He should seek deliberately to extend his knowledge, and to cultivate his powers of discernment by the careful study of the members of his class, not forgetting, in the midst of his serious occupation, the saving salt of humour. When he

very loosely used. Teachers are urged to make their lessons " interesting "—an adjective, by the way, with a much less firm content of meaning than " interest " itself. The injunction is true if it means that the teacher must somehow make it really worth while to listen and to participate actively in a lesson. But it is not true if it implies that he must use any and all means to capture the fleeting attention of a class, and so to produce a superficial and momentary " interest " in what is not really pertinent or useful. The interest the teacher must evoke is that of intelligent co-operation in something that is worth doing and has to be done. The motives behind the interest may not always be the highest, but vigorous work, even in the lessons where drudgery is inevitable, is impossible without interest. What is suggested later, in the chapters on method and procedure in teaching, is all aimed at securing this right and essential kind of interest.

Another psychological term which the teacher is sure to meet in any reading about teaching at the present day is " instinct." Certain thinkers use this attribute as a starting point in considering psychology in relation to society, and, under society, to education. The beginner, however, need not be greatly concerned with theories of instinct, or attempt deliberately to encourage some instincts as such and to control others. It is enough for him to know that in fact children are curious and inquisitive, that they show fear and timidity at times, and at other times are bold and enterprising, combative, self-assertive and even conceited ; that they can be induced to attack a task as something to be overcome, that they are usually fond of the company of their fellow creatures, and willingly join in common activities in the classroom and in the field. Of these characteristics he should be aware and be able to detect them when they show themselves, and he will soon learn by experience which are to be utilised as a help and which must be checked when they seem likely to hinder the work.

In no part of a school is the necessity for close observation of children more desirable than in classes of very young children. Happily the women who teach these, and the governesses who teach young children at home, are usually well qualified for the task by native sympathy and understanding. If they are not naturally attracted towards children of nursery or kindergarten age, towards what, in the elementary schools, have been called Infants, they had better seek another occupation, or at any rate, confine themselves to teaching older girls and boys.

The differences between children, which to some extent become blurred as they reach boyhood and girlhood proper, are patent when they are young, and these differences call for differences of treatment. The teacher will meet with all kinds. The shy and timid child will require gentle encouragement, the pert and forward checks and rebukes. The sluggish must be gradually bustled a little, the restless provided with occupation which will keep her quietly busy, the talkative must be taught to talk at the right and not at the wrong time, the silent enticed into speech, and so on. The child who is clumsy with fingers must be helped and " shown how," and her opposite given scope for her nimbleness. The young teacher must learn to distinguish between positive untruthfulness and statements which are due to active imagination, no easy task when children are too young to know the boundaries of exaggeration and falsehood. The quick child must be allowed the advantage of his quickness, provided that this does not lead to exhaustion or to an unhealthy stimulation. The slow child is a problem, wherever he is encountered. To hurry him when he is young is fatal, but he must not be merely given up in despair. He is probably slow in some ways and quick in others, and praise judiciously bestowed upon his success on one side will lead him to persevere on others.

Two more general observations are appropriate here. Many modern writers on childhood lay stress upon the outstanding importance of the early years in the process of education. They tell us that inborn tendencies, good and bad alike, are so much strengthened and confirmed in the early years that they can hardly be changed afterwards. Habits are formed which can be subsequently eradicated only with difficulty. The obvious duty of those who are in charge of young children, parents or teachers, is to encourage the good tendencies and habits and to check those which may become dangerous. Happily for the responsibility of

teachers and for those who advise teachers, the
mischief, if any, is said to be done in the earliest
years, before children come to school. Whether
this is so or not, watchfulness on the part of teachers
is imperative.

We are warned particularly by the writers
mentioned against what they call " repression."
The " repression " to be avoided is the unwarrant-
able discouragement of natural propensities, which
sometimes should be satisfied outright and sometimes guided into other more useful channels.
Children are naturally curious, and enterprising by
nature: they wish to know, and to try in all sorts
of fields. " See what Tommy is doing and tell
him not to," says the foolish mother in *Punch*.
That is unwise " repression " : Tommy should be
given something that he may safely do, and
" safely " does not mean merely that he is not to
trouble the repose of a selfish household.

One distinguished philosopher urges, with much
force and eloquence, that " fear " should be
eliminated in the training of young children, because
" fear " used to impose repressions from outside
may result in unhealthy self-repressions later. This
is worth thinking over.

A child should never be repressed save for some
good reason, the comfort of the rest of the class,
the desirability that he should, in his own interest,
cease to do what he is doing, or that he may escape
a positive and threatened danger. With every
wish to satisfy the inquiries of an inquisitive and
persistent child in a class the teacher must refuse

if, by giving way, the proper claims of the rest are neglected. Experience, coupled with intelligence and sympathy, will bring the power to secure orderliness without undue repression.

The second general observation bears upon play. Teachers are urged to teach through play, because playing is so essentially a child's life and business. This counsel needs to be examined with some care. The joyous activities of a thoroughly well-conducted kindergarten or infant class are both work and play, and the teacher of young children need not be too scrupulous in trying to distinguish between them. The children themselves will not distinguish. Therefore she need not appeal to the children to enter upon some task on the plea that it is play. If they are attracted and interested, it is play, or as good as play. To speak of " playing at shop " in an early lesson in simple numbers is right enough, but to introduce an artificial game in dealing, for example, with the alphabet or the composition of syllables is foolishness. A teacher who is afraid to enter on a lesson except under the pretence that it is play, is probably trying to teach her class something they are not yet ready to learn.

On the other hand when the class has heard a story, and they wish to " play " it, the idea is sound enough, for children not only enjoy simple dramatising of all sorts, but find in it a means by which to satisfy their natural need for " expressing," as it is called, " impressions " which they have received. Play which is of the right kind and free from any artificial element has the very great advantage of providing ready-made the opportunities which a teacher should always be seeking, for letting the class really share in the lesson, and not merely listen or work by themselves. Its importance in affording practice and training in speech has only to be mentioned to be perceived.

We may now pass to the positive contributions which psychology has made to teaching, those which the beginner should know. For the most part they will be found to be confirmations of what wise and observant teachers have themselves discovered. At any rate, in so far as they run counter to traditional opinion and practice, they are outside the sphere in which the beginner works, since they concern the major questions of curriculum and organisation which are settled for the beginner in teaching before he enters the school. In this chapter attention can be called only to a few general points ; but the particular suggestions in later chapters can also all be supported by arguments from the science of mind as well as by actual experience. Many of these general points will appear to be commonplaces ; it is, however, unfortunately true that they are only too frequently forgotten or neglected.

Psychologists and physiologists have developed the idea of growth, and have attempted to define accurately several well-marked stages in the early development of the human being. These stages are, roughly : childhood, boyhood or girlhood, and youth. Thus in modern applications of the science of mind to education we find stress laid upon the idea of the child as a growing organism. We were formerly apt to assume that all minds were inert tablets upon which life's experiences, including education, made impressions ; or, alternatively, that the mind of the young child was a receptacle for information merely requiring to be filled. In theorising on the subject, immaturity was often forgotten and the valuable conception of " stages in growth " overlooked.

In its bare form this biological conception, useful to keep in mind, is not of much practical importance to the beginner. Some of its corollaries, however, are important. Growth is not uniform ; all the individuals of a species do not advance at precisely the same rate, nor does the individual plant or animal itself always grow at the same speed throughout. This irregularity applies to mental as well as to physical growth. Accordingly the teacher must not be surprised to find pupils of the same age and from similar surroundings differing very greatly, some being precociously advanced and others unaccountably slow. Also he will find that a pupil who has made rapid progress for some time will suddenly appear to come to a standstill. The teacher should be prepared to allow for these peculiarities, to take advantage of a spurt by his pupil, and to be patient when progress appears to be slow. All this is simple common sense ; but a beginner in teaching will not always be able to distinguish between real and assumed slowness, and between the slacking which is due to indolence and the retardation which the pupil cannot help.

What has just been said on the teacher's duty
of observing the members of his class as individuals
and of learning how they can be dealt with as
individuals applies also to classes of children, but
the conditions are different. By the time they are
eight or nine years of age, children are usually
grouped in classes with a settled programme of
work. So, though the special peculiarities of
individuals will be embarrassing enough at times,
they tend to be obscured by the general temper
and attitude of the whole class. The differences
remain, but they show themselves as differences in
ability, intelligence, power of application and in
rate of progress, rather than as differences of
temperament.

The young teacher especially will be preoccupied
with his task of leading a very mixed team over
the same ground at a pace which is not too breathless
for the slow and not too tedious for the quick. He
will have to exercise all his wits to distinguish those
of his pupils who are really dull of comprehension
and who learn very slowly from those who are
merely indolent and do not trouble to pull their
weight. With the first he will deal tenderly, with
the second relentlessly. Even the intelligent, he
will find, have periods when their progress slackens
and when, as it were, they need time to get their
breath again. For as we have said most children
advance not at an even rate, but in fits and starts.

The teacher need not worry greatly about this,
provided he can be sure of discovering wilful and
unnecessary slackness, and provided that he can

give to the brighter portion of his class work which will occupy them usefully while he is attending to the duller members. When he has gained a reasonable control of his class and is no longer engaged in the first business of securing discipline, he can profitably study the various modes by which skilful teachers keep both the quick and the slow busily at work. One of the aims of what is known as the Dalton plan is to meet this universal difficulty arising from different rates at which children work and learn. A teacher who is not in a position to adopt the Dalton plan in full may usefully employ some of the features of the method, applying them with the modifications demanded by his special circumstances. If discouragement arises over very slow progress, the beginner may take heart and remember that as a rough rule, what is learnt slowly is often retained more firmly than what is acquired rapidly.

The very slow pupil, the dunce of the older days, is always a problem. This is the boy or girl who, without being really deficient as a human being, seems to be excessively stupid ; he reads haltingly, writes badly, cannot spell, cannot remember how to work a sum and invariably gets it wrong ; the knowledge he absorbs in geography, history, grammar and the like, is casual, inaccurate and confused. Sometimes, especially with girls, but boys are also to be found in this category, the dunce is quite good on the language side; reads, writes and speaks well but breaks down wholly on the mathematical side.

It has to be sadly confessed that the all-round dunce is out of place in the ordinary school, almost the whole of the teaching in which is literary and academic. His interests—and this applies just as much to girls—are not what is commonly called intellectual. Very often the slowness and confusion is due to bad training in early years ; reading, which to the average child offers no insuperable difficulties, is to him a mechanical art, and he has not been adequately drilled in the mechanics ; his arithmetic is spoiled not so much by his dullness as by bad foundations in the earliest stages—he has never been practised enough in addition and subtraction and in the multiplication table ; the lessons in geography and history have not awakened his imagination to their delights, for his imagination is busy with other things.

The dunce is an interesting study and usually has redeeming points, which the teacher should be alert enough to see. Of these redeeming points the teacher should take the utmost advantage. The dunce is often very practical, able to do things with hands and fingers, and probably, if a boy, really interested in machines and things that work ; if a girl, fond of sewing, cookery, of being busy with children and of managing generally. Both may be good at games, and more at ease out of doors than in the classroom ; they may be not only good sportsmen and good sportswomen in the making, but also good naturalists and botanists. The teacher's duty is twofold : to seize or devise possible opportunities of using such abilities as these children

c

often have ; and to lead them to see that success in what they are really interested in can be secured only if they will be at the trouble to gain mastery over the necessary elements of learning. Even the beginner in teaching should remember, as a sobering check upon his natural enthusiasm for learning, that it is often found that boys and girls who are apparently dull at school are able to achieve success in after life, where their practical intelligence and their concealed ability have fuller scope than they have in the ordinary school.

The treatment of children who are backward or deficient in a medical sense is not properly within the province of the young teacher. The " backward " are those who are naturally not deficient but for some reason have been unable to make the progress that their age would lead one to expect. The ordinary slow child is of course " backward " in one sense : but where there is a wide gap between age and attainment, after the stage of childhood proper, it is for the head master or head mistress to advise.

So also with " mentally deficient " children. These are children in whose mental make up there is something wanting—wanting, and not merely undeveloped. Broadly speaking, without special training they will be unable to take a proper place after school in industrial or even home life ; and even with special training, can do so only under kindly supervision and control. This is primarily a medical matter. The beginner may be cautioned against condemning too hastily a child who is merely

slow, or backward in the sense just described as
" mentally deficient." He will be generally safe
in giving these unfortunates the benefit of the
doubt, but if they are really deficient he cannot
deal with them. The teacher who wishes further
to investigate the questions raised in the foregoing
will find material in books mentioned in a later
chapter

CHAPTER IV

IT may be thought that with the extensive medical service under Education Authorities the concern of the teacher, and of the young teacher in particular, with school hygiene is very slight. A little reflection, however, will show that such an idea is mistaken. It is true that the teacher cannot alter the structure of the school, and that only rarely can he have a voice in the selection of the furniture of his classroom, although both may affect the health of his pupils. But he has duties in the sphere of health none the less. They are duties, moreover, which call for no special medical knowledge, but require only ordinary vigilance and common sense. They may now be briefly sketched.

The classroom and its main equipment have to be taken as they are found. There will presumably be means of ventilation, by windows, and perhaps by special contrivances. It is the teacher's business to know what these means are, and to see that they are used. Cross-ventilation, that is, the free passage of air from outside through the room and out again, is the best kind of ventilation when possible. Where there are windows which open on two sides, preferably opposite sides, of a room, a sort of natural ventilation occurs which needs little attention from the teacher, when the windows are open. But such rooms are not too common. Even in them, if the window openings are too high, there is apt to be a well of stagnant air about the desks where the children sit. If they are too low, the constant draught may be dangerous to weakly children not inured to working in a breeze.

The teacher will have to adjust the inlets according to the weather, and to the susceptibility of his class. A combination of open window and open door is not to be advised. The door cannot be left open always because of the need for quiet, and children sitting near an open door are in a direct draught which is more dangerous to many persons than a general and light current of air circulating freely. More care will be needed where the main openings are on one side only. Some modern schools have " French " windows or windows which open wholly on swivels ; when these are open the room is almost in the open air. Other rooms have sash windows with hoppers : the sash can be raised and the hoppers kept open practically all the year round. This arrangement provides at least a good second rate system of ventilation. It secures, as do the other devices, that movement of air which it is now believed to be more important than the maintenance of exactly right proportions of oxygen and the rest.

In spite of all efforts, the atmosphere of the ordinary schoolroom will be more or less vitiated after a lesson, and it will be well to flush the room with air, if possible after every lesson, but at any rate at the recreation interval. A little vigorous physical exercise while windows are open to the widest will not only prevent any danger of catching cold but will be a relief and a refreshment to the pupils. Where the children are old enough, it is a good plan to appoint ventilation monitors with well-defined duties. The young teacher will not be responsible for school cleaning. But he can minimise dust by care in the use of chalk and duster, and, through monitors again, he can ensure that paper and litter are not allowed on the desks and floor, and that cupboards are tidy and clean. The main responsibility for tidiness and freedom from dust should rest upon the children, the teacher being careful to set a good example.

The heating of the room, also, will be more or less out of the control of the teacher, especially where there is a central system. If there are radiators he should know how they work, and whether he has means of regulating them. He should report any conspicuous failure to heat the room. If there are fires, he will probably be responsible for them, once they are lit, and this duty should never be delegated to a young child without full precautions against danger. Special measures are sometimes necessary in excessively cold or excessively hot weather ; occasionally the time table may have to be modified.

All these attentions increase the comfort of both teacher and class, and add to the efficiency of the teaching. A failure to take account of them will mean for both lethargy and somnolence, or restlessness, irritability and inattention. The teacher need not be fussy, but he should be vigilant.

More important in their bearing upon individual children are certain precautions to be observed affecting personal hygiene. These relate mostly to the way the pupils sit or stand, and to the ease with which they see and hear. There is also something to be said on the detection of disease, and the signs of fatigue.

The children should sit in a good light which is diffused but not dazzling. In an ordinary room, with the class arranged in rows, the best light is from the left. This is because, in ordinary circumstances, pupils use the right hand in writing and thus where the left side is not shadowed the words last written are easily seen. Front light may dazzle the front row and it casts a shadow on those behind. Light from the back is the worst, since it throws the pupils' work into shadow and is trying to the teacher's eyes. The teacher will probably find the desks arranged for lighting from the left, but there may be comparatively dark places, and he should put no pupils there if he can avoid it. He should also use the artificial light sensibly, putting it on at the right time and rearranging the pupils where necessary. If the class is very small, and the room is well lighted, these

" rules " may be superfluous, but they should be kept in mind.

Apart from these general precautions, the teacher should not fail to notice any peculiarities of sight in particular children. Some children, especially those who are short-sighted, tend to bring the reading book they are using nearer and nearer to their eyes, and in writing to bring their faces nearer and nearer to the desk. For normal eyes a distance of about 12 inches between eye and book is held to be best. But it would be improper for the inexperienced teacher to impose any fixed rule. Where a child seems to have the book too near, he should be asked if he finds it equally comfortable to read with the book farther away. If he does, he should be encouraged to keep the book at the proper distance and not to bring it nearer.

In the same way the habit of writing with the face very near the desk or with the head aslant should be checked in the first instance to ascertain if it is merely a piece of carelessness ; if it persists, the teacher should take steps to obtain the opinion of the school doctor. In both reading and writing lessons the teacher should try to judge whether an apparently unhealthy position is due to weakness or is only an uncorrected habit. He will soon discover those pupils who cannot easily read what is on the blackboard or see clearly a map, diagram or picture. They should be brought into a position from which they can see. It is obvious also that all writing, figures, diagrams or sketches on the blackboard should be bold and clear enough to be read or seen with ease by all the class.

There is little to be said about hearing except that those who may be a little deaf should be well to the front. The teacher can do no more than report cases of deafness. Neither as to ears nor eyes must he make recommendations to the pupil himself, except as suggested above. As has been said before, the teacher must speak slowly and without shouting, but so distinctly as to be properly heard by all. It is not often realised how soon listeners tire of trying to make sense of what is uttered indistinctly or rapidly, or how nerves are jarred by a continuous bellow of speech.

Position in sitting is not at all easy to deal with. A rigid uniformity is most undesirable, for, among other reasons, the seats and desks in a classroom are usually of the same measurements and the pupils of a class are never of one size. Twisted positions, especially if they are adopted in order to secure a better light, clearly call for attention. Doctors warn us that curvature of the spine may follow protracted unhealthy positions. Good modern desks are furnished with back rests, the purpose of which is not to repose the back so much as to give it support in attitudes which in schools cannot be frequently changed.

The main point of importance in relation to sitting is that the pupil should sit comfortably, without such uneasiness as will distract his mind from whatever he is doing ; neither lounging nor lolling, nor taking up a stiff " drill " position on occasions which do not call for drill. If he is comfortable, hands and feet will look after themselves. Children can be told not to bend or crouch when sitting to listen ; when they are writing or drawing, they should be encouraged to keep their backs straight.

Certain old-fashioned attitudes are now discredited. Constant folding of arms narrows the chest, and the " neck-rest," where the head is held by clasped hands, is a part of physical exercises, but not a position to be maintained for long. " Hands on heads " as a command is stupid, an admission of failure in discipline, imposing a strain which is of no value as exercise and almost certainly hurtful. Many of the difficulties and certain of the present dangers to health arise from the practice of using standard desks. Chairs and tables, of sizes varied to suit different sizes of children, would be far better.

An important part of the teacher's duty, as now conceived, especially in schools under a public authority, is to look out for signs of ill-health or disease and report in the first instance to the head of the school. The observant teacher will not be slow to detect evidence of weak sight, of deafness, and of a generally enfeebled condition, but he must not presume to make a diagnosis or do more than state clearly what he has observed and what he suspects. The importance of noting early the signs of infectious ailments need not be emphasised. For such signs the reader is referred to books dealing especially with health in schools.

The detection of fatigue is a less skilled matter, though the books upon health in school will furnish details and symptoms which would not be noted by an ordinary observer. The obvious result of fatigue, plain to any teacher, will be an unmistakable failure in attention and in briskness. If they have been working vigorously during a period, a class may be expected to be healthily tired at the end. But the fatigue for which the teacher should be on the look out is something different. It will be shown by individual pale faces and strained looks, by limpness of raised hands and by general lassitude. Where the teacher has reason to suppose that a child is in reality more fatigued than he should be, he had better bring the matter to the notice of the head of the school. The class as a whole, if fatigued, will be restless and inattentive, will answer questions in a listless and an erratic way, will yawn and lounge.

General fatigue at the wrong time may be due to causes, many of which it is in the teacher's power to remove. The ventilation may be bad or the class may have been too long in one position, sitting or standing. Very often they are fatigued because the lesson is monotonous, the teacher talking too much or too long at a time or in a dull manner, while the class has nothing to do but listen. Less often, except with delicate children, is fatigue due to the length of the lessons or to an unusual demand on their brains. Young teachers should bear in mind that in an ordinary lesson covering an ordinary period in a time-table, children are never working at full pressure all the time. They tend to work in spurts, with keen attention for a period and with attention relaxed at times, though by no means lost, and with, no doubt, occasional moments of complete inattention unseen by the teacher. Few children could work for a whole morning at their highest power without feeling the strain, as those teachers know who teach keen children privately.

Those who are in charge of very small classes, or governesses who have only one or two children to look after, should bear this in mind. For them short periods of "intense" concentration should be succeeded by intervals for physical movement, or by lessons when the speed is, as it were, on a lower gear. This is not to suggest that the pupils should have an easy time and be spared real exertion and real work. But some eager teachers with eager and responsive pupils fail to realise that they may over-excite the children when a class is small, by making too prolonged a demand upon their interest and attention. For many young children whose home lives tend to make them overstrung, a sedative type of teaching, with periods when they are not being stimulated, may be recommended. Such periods may be introduced without risk of encouraging mental torpor. The conditions under which many larger classes are taught make this warning less appropriate for such classes, unless the children are very young. But for classes of all sorts, teachers will do well to consider the advantage of so combining a more stimulating with a less stimulating kind of teaching so as to prevent both boredom and restless excitement.

The teacher should not, of course, neglect his own health. Apart from advice on personal hygiene which it is beyond the province of this book to give, it may be suggested that the teacher may discover the causes of his own fatigue among those already mentioned as creating fatigue in his class. It is possible for teachers to be too eager and excited for their own good or that of the class ; to use the voice to the point of exhaustion, to forget that real teaching does not consist in carrying the whole burden on their own shoulders, but in causing the pupils to learn and work for themselves. It is the teacher's duty to be an example of mental and physical fitness. Both may be gained by regular and fit practice. On the physical side the young teacher should take as much exercise as possible in the open air, and adopt a scheme of regular bodily training which can be continued when vigorous games are no longer possible. Such a scheme may be devised from the Syllabus of Physical Training, issued by the Board of Education.

CHAPTER V

THE young teacher must expect to find that his fitness for the work is measured at first mainly by his power of keeping a class under control. Many an eager and enthusiastic beginner has found his ardour quenched and his expectations defeated merely because a group of small children would not behave decorously under his eye. Their refusal to accept from him either instruction or admonishment makes him a mere cipher so far as class teaching is concerned. Worse still, it makes him a useless and unprofitable member of the staff team. The unfortunate colleagues who are called upon to take over a form or class which has spent a period in boisterous ragging have just grounds of complaint, while the head master is naturally concerned, and inclined to impatience, when he sees that his plans for the whole school are being imperilled by reason of a teacher's failure to make the first step towards good craftsmanship. It is obvious that nobody—however gifted in respect of knowledge or well versed in the essential principles of craft—can teach pupils who will neither listen to him nor pay any respect to his learning. The unhappy fate of such weak aspirants may be a rapid sequence of posts and premature retirement from the work in which they might have succeeded had they been able to control a group of children.

It is well for the beginner to understand that while the individual child may be a delightful creature he—or she—may be very troublesome in a class. Mob sentiment is proverbial, but it is seldom so ruthless as when displayed by a class of boys or girls who are completely out of hand. The weak disciplinarian is a pitiable spectacle as he vainly endeavours to quell the turbulence, and restrain the unbridled efforts of his tormentors. For he is beyond human aid. The head master or a minatory colleague may come to his help now and again, but these extraneous efforts are only transient in their effects, for nobody can keep discipline at second-hand. It must be the result of the teacher's own personality, supported by an intuitive or acquired skill in maintaining at least the outward shows of order.

Let it be understood here that these outward shows are not the whole of the matter. True discipline is something more than decorum, although seemly conduct is one of its outward and visible signs. The inward grace which alone deserves the name of discipline, and should be the teacher's aim, is the power of self-control. The best form of order in a class is that maintained by the pupils themselves as the result of individual self-respect and self-restraint, fortified by public opinion in the group and in the school, and aided by the respect which a teacher should be able to command. When the teacher finds that order of this kind prevails in his class he may justly feel that he has passed through the apprentice and even the journeyman stage and has reached the position of a master craftsman.

Besides the overt and premeditated indiscipline just described there is a kind of indiscipline which manifests itself in slackness and inattention. The force of school tradition and the general goodwill of the class, or at least the absence of any disposition to annoy the young teacher, may preclude concerted disorder. But in the absence of the easy control of the skilled practitioner there is room for the more elusive forms of indiscipline. There may be some pupils who are positively inclined to laziness and shirking while others, often even the best, will take advantage of a weak or an unskilful teacher and relapse into slackness and talkativeness. There is no deliberate " ca' canny " strike, but a general relapse into carelessness. The best safeguard against such a relapse is for the teacher to have his lessons carefully prepared. As will be shown later method and discipline are closely connected. Loose and uncertain method and want of adequate preparation are direct incitements to inattention, while a well prepared teacher will keep his class so much engaged that they have no time for wandering. Besides this, the young teacher must train himself to vigilance and be prompt in checking incipient inattention and restlessness. This involves in the first place the gaining of power to see the whole of

the class and letting the class know that he has
them under his eye. A young teacher is apt to
concentrate his attention upon the front row or
the centre of the class and to overlook the antics
of those who are not immediately under his notice.
Secondly, until he has established his own discipline, he had better be a martinet in small matters,
not by trying to be bullying or harsh, but by insisting upon strict obedience to his instructions and
commands. Interruptions, answering out of turn,
furtive whisperings and promptings, fidgetings must
be checked promptly.

In order to cope with the carelessness and slackness in work which result from inattention and un-
checked indolence the teacher must adopt the same
attitude as is suggested in regard to premeditated
ragging. He should display no outward sign of
disturbance, but quietly and firmly demand the
complete fulfilment of every task. It will soon be
found by the culprits that on the whole it is better
to attend carefully to the instruction and to perform
their exercises properly since any failure merely
adds to their labours in the long run. The teacher
must be quietly alert in detecting those who are
deliberately trying his powers in this regard. He
should take pains to ensure that their exercises are
carefully examined and that every failure to do
good work is promptly visited with a demand for
another and more satisfactory attempt. For the
slacker the standard in these second and third
attempts should be even higher than that for the
ordinary conscientious and painstaking pupil, since

D

our aim is to bring home to the culprit the knowledge that idleness and inattention involve penalties beyond mere reparation. This is a lesson worth learning since it has applications to life outside school.

The foregoing suggestions apply to classes where the children are old enough for the class teaching usual in schools. In classes of the youngest children a freer kind of discipline is encouraged, the methods of which can be learnt best by observing a skilled teacher at work. She will be found to engage the right degree of attention to her and to their work by quietly keeping the children busy, by gently suppressing those who claim too much notice and by those arts of pleasant cajolery which a good teacher of very young children has at her command.

In practice it oftens happens that teachers are satisfied when they have achieved the power of maintaining order by a system of restraints, backed up by force or supported by such external devices as good and bad marks, with minor punishments. Order thus maintained may gain for the teacher a reputation as a good disciplinarian, but in the true educational sense he is not so much a real disciplinarian as a drill sergeant, and it may well happen that his pupils are so preoccupied with fulfilling his demands for outwardly good order that they have little energy left for the business of learning or for that inner discipline to which we have referred.

Moreover, it is found that school discipline based solely on restraints from outside tends to become nothing more than a school habit or set of habits, practised by the pupil in the schoolroom, so long as the teacher, a kind of Ancient Mariner, " holds him with his glittering eye," but discarded promptly when school is over.

The failure of such discipline is illustrated if we consider the case of a convict who spends years, it may be, under complete restraint. During this period, long or short, he is uniformly punctual, honest, clean and tidy, an abstainer from alcohol and tobacco, a regular churchgoer, an early riser and one who works without intermission if with little zest. Viewed through the eyes of the drill disciplinarian he is a model of decorum. Yet it is often found that within forty-eight hours of his release from the outward restraints, he has broken every one of the rules that he kept while in prison. His decorum was of the gaol, and it broke down in the freer atmosphere of ordinary civic life.

Sometimes we find in school a discipline that will not function beyond the school walls. To the extent that it fails in this by so much is it falling short of the ideal. A school does not exist for the sole purpose of being in itself a good school, but for the further and greater purpose of training children for social life outside. Care should be taken to secure, as far as possible, that all items of its building plan, structure, equipment and routine are not such as will create in the child's mind the impression that school is a place insulated from the everyday outside world, with its separate code of conduct and separate body of experiences, neither of which can be carried over into ordinary life without great adjustment.

The young teacher can play but a small part in securing all this, but he can at least see to it that in his own classroom an effort is made to avoid artificial conventions and restraints. He may base his class discipline upon the general requirements of courtesy, fair dealing, mutual consideration, and that give-and-take which is demanded of all members of a group engaged in a co-operative enterprise. These qualities are called for in every kind of undertaking, from the conduct of a football match to the management of municipal and national affairs. In the classroom they may be practised and rehearsed in the certainty that the discipline thus engendered will have a lasting effect, since it will not be out of harmony with the practice of life outside the school.

We may now consider in more detail some of the devices which a beginner may find useful. These are not put forward as infallible prescriptions, for in all its aspects teaching is a craft which depends on the power of the individual to adapt general principles to his own circumstances. Were it otherwise teaching would be " a dull mechanic art." It would call for no skill or intelligence beyond that required to comprehend and apply rigid rules and ready made " schemes " and " hints " such as are purveyed for those teachers who seek to be absolved from the labour of thinking out their own problems. All that is here attempted or desired is to set forth some broad principles which experience has shown to be generally valid.

Of these the first is that children prefer order to disorder. This preference reveals itself even in infancy, for the youngest child seems to relish routine, and to dislike a breach of continuity in his accustomed way of life. He will demand that a story, when repeated to him, shall be framed in the words first employed, and he will protest if familiar experiences lack anything of their accustomed background. All this is probably due to the working of the instinct of self-preservation which leads to a shrinking from the unknown or unfamiliar as a possible source of danger. Among adults the instinct must be curbed and even checked, and it is part of the task of the schools to remove the paralysing effects of fear, whether it be fear of new experiences or the more insidious and crippling fear of new ideas.

The young teacher, however, may take courage from the thought that the majority of those in his class will be ready to support him if he shows firmness and good sense in maintaining order. If, on the other hand, he is weak and foolish they will not hesitate to torment him without mercy. In his first dealings with a class, therefore, the teacher should exhibit a quiet determination to maintain control. Let him say as little as possible at first, giving necessary orders in an easy manner, and with the evident expectation of seeing them carried out promptly. Above all he should refrain from barking at the class, or telling them that he means to have order, or becoming visibly perturbed when his first commands are not obeyed as he would wish.

Children are wonderfully and disquietingly quick in detecting any sign of nervousness in a new teacher, and they find a mischievous pleasure in playing upon it. The teacher's best defence is to be imperturbable, and somewhat reticent even under provocation. Instead of hurling fiery rebukes, or threats and remonstrances, he should remain calm and silent, as if he were surprised rather than vexed. This attitude has the result of making the class feel that he may have unsuspected reserves of power. In the American phrase, the teacher keeps them guessing, and all the prudent ones will play for safety rather than run the risk of unknown perils.

There may be a few enterprising spirits who show a disposition to discover the limits of the teacher's patience. It is best to apply some device which will make them uneasy without disclosing a penalty. Thus they may be asked to come forward one at a time and write down their full names and addresses on a sheet of paper. Having done this they will be told to return to their places, and it is certain that they will do so with some little anxiety as to what may happen. This anxiety should not be appeased until the end of the period, when the teacher may tell them, crisply and briefly, that their misconduct was noted and that any future pranks will be treated seriously. No specific threat is needed. It is enough for them to realise that they are dealing with a teacher who will stand no nonsense. They had best be kept guessing as to the precise nature of a possible explosion.

This procedure during the first period with a class will go far to establish the teacher's position. It is the first period which counts for most, since a blunder or failure in class management at the outset may have enduring ill-results, and possibly prevent the teacher from ever getting on terms with that particular group of pupils. Let us repeat that this first approach should be unmarked by any sign of nervousness on the part of the teacher, still less by any display of truculence or suggestion that trouble is expected. Teacher and pupils should meet as strangers who are on the threshold of better acquaintance and of later friendship. A little reticence is desirable at this stage, and it is especially so on the part of the teacher.

We have said that youngsters prefer to be kept in order, but it has been urged also that all true discipline involves readiness to learn. The teacher must play his part in this by having the subject-matter so fully mastered in his own mind and so well-arranged either in memory or lesson notes that no time is wasted. Uncertainty as to the facts or as to the next step in a lesson will lead to those fumbling pauses which are positive inducements to disorder. This means, in effect, that the teacher must discipline himself before he aspires to discipline his pupils. If he expects them to be orderly in demeanour he must be himself orderly in mind. If he looks for industry and restraint in them he must practise industry in preparing his lessons and restraint in dealing with vexatious incidents.

By degrees the preliminary reticence which has been advised may be allowed to yield to mutual understanding, and even to a kind of friendship. But it is a mistake to aim at being an elder brother or a " pal." These are not patriarchal days, and nobody has a classroomful of younger brothers all of about the same age. Nor is it possible for a grown man to be the " pal " of a group of boys, especially of boys whom he has to teach. In time he may win their regard and even affection, but he must above all gain their respect. Given this, he will have little difficulty with discipline at any stage or in any circumstances.

It must not be supposed that precisely the same method will serve at every stage and under all conditions. Thus, discipline in a very small class presents its own special difficulties. Many students in training and many young teachers who are able to control a class of thirty or more are somewhat non-plussed when confronted by a class of one-third that size. The regimental method tends to break down in the small group because the pupils forget that they are in a class, with others to be considered. They will interrupt the lesson, or clamour for individual attention when they are engaged in a task. The teacher's best course is to prepare work enough to keep everybody busy, having special regard to the more irrepressible spirits, and those who can finish an exercise very quickly. With a small group there is scope for attention to individual needs, the fostering of individual interests, and the encouragement of progress at the pupil's own rate. All of these are difficult to attain with a large class.

On the other hand it should be remembered that children are gregarious creatures, and that they enjoy group exercises, such as singing, dancing, drill, games and co-operative handwork, and they like to hear a good class lesson on history or geography. Even in a small group there should be contrived as much opportunity as possible for such exercises. In a larger class the need will be to guard against the danger of keeping the quicker children on the curb while the slower ones overtake them. Forethought will be called for, and supplementary work should be ready for those who can accomplish the average task more quickly than the rest.

It should be noted that the arrangement of the time-table may have very important effects on discipline. Lessons should be so distributed as to allow for a judicious mingling of relatively strenuous work calling for close attention and mental effort with exercises which are comparatively restful or which demand a different form of activity. A tired child will often be petulant and troublesome, and the teacher should never forget that the process of formal learning is full of difficulties for the young mind. The pupil becomes fretted and uneasy if the pace is too fast or if the teacher shows undue impatience.

It was well said by Dr. Jowett, the famous Master of Balliol, that in learning we might find that twice two made four but that twice four often made only two. Remembering this, the young teacher will refrain from expecting his pupils to accomplish the impossible by learning at once everything that he puts before them. Patient repetition and a slow progress are inevitable accompaniments of all sound instruction, for the true student belongs to the order of ruminants. He must have time to chew the cud of knowledge before he can assimilate it. Repetition and slow progress, however, must not involve tedium. Thus, when a rule or a formula has been learned and understood as far as is needed for an immediate purpose it should not be merely reiterated again and again. True assimilation will call for a revision which will present the same truth in varied forms and applications. The process helps discipline by minimising the dullness of learning, and by keeping the minds of the pupils active, so that they feel themselves usefully occupied and have no desire to waste time or indulge in mischief.

There are specific aids to discipline which call for brief mention. In former days the chief ally of a teacher was held to be the fear of physical pain, but this method of maintaining discipline is becoming discredited. Without seeking to deny that there are occasions when corporal punishment may be the best method of checking certain forms of misbehaviour, we suggest that it should not be employed without careful consideration, and due regard to the nature of the offence. It should never be used indiscriminately, or as an expression of a teacher's impatience. The boxing of ears and indiscriminate slapping are positive hindrances to discipline since they show that the teacher lacks self-control. The only occasions when corporal punishment can be justified are those on which misbehaviour takes the form of physical bullying of weaker fellow pupils or the kind of obstinate refusal to obey orders which is sometimes shown by children who glory in notoriety. In such cases a dose of physical pain, judiciously administered, may serve to check bullying or impertinence, and even help the pupil to brace himself against his own faults.

Weakness in discipline, which is manifested in unpunctual or unsatisfactory work, is best dealt with on the principle that a bond must be fulfilled. Thus, instead of inflicting a penalty which has no relation to the offence, such as the learning or writing of lines, it is better to require the completion of the working-time and the satisfactory performance of the task. When it is once understood that the time lost at the beginning of the day must be made up later, and that careless work will involve the whole task being done over again, the pupil soon discovers that it is more convenient to observe rules than to break them.

The discipline of a school or a class depends very largely upon the general tone of the community. By tone is meant the customary and spontaneous behaviour of everybody, including pupils and teachers. Where this is marked by the qualities which we associate with pleasant social relationships, the tone is good, for misdemeanours will not occur since they are so unusual as to be unexpected. They are as we say " bad form," and for that reason will be avoided. It should be the teacher's aim to develop an atmosphere of good form, and to play his own part in maintaining it. The essential basis is that of Justice. Everybody should feel that he will receive fair and considerate treatment, and he should realise that he is expected to show the same treatment to others.

Although competition among children acts as a great stimulus to learning, it may also be a source of discontent and ill-feeling. Sometimes there has been tried with success a plan by which pupils are not placed in a comparative order of merit, but are merely told how far they have advanced or receded as individuals from the standard reached in the first exercise of the week or of the term. The teacher assigns a mark to each of these first exercises, but he does not disclose it. When the next exercise is marked, he issues a list showing, with the aid of plus and minus signs, the gain or loss in marks of each pupil, and the order of merit is not published until the end of the week or of the term. This method has the advantage of removing one cause of friction between the pupils, and the discontent with the teacher which is often felt where a boy or girl feels that an exercise has not received proper credit.

This point of technique is mentioned merely to illustrate the fact that class discipline and class tone are resultants of many forces, and not, as is often supposed, solely the outcome of vigorous personality in the teacher, supported by rigid routine. We should remind ourselves that discipline in the literal sense is the attitude which becomes a disciple and our aim should be to develop in our pupils an eagerness to learn from us, and a disposition to permit their fellows to do the same.

CHAPTER VI

GENERAL PRINCIPLES OF TEACHING—I

THE three essentials of teaching as craftsmanship are knowledge, method and discipline. The teacher must know what he is to teach, must be able to present it in the best way, and must control his pupils so that they may respond to his teaching. Though the three essentials may be kept distinct for the purpose of discussing them in detail, they are in fact closely connected and interwoven. If the teacher has his own knowledge well arranged, he is already on the way to a good mode of imparting it. Sound method is a potent help in class control, for a class is ready to respect and to listen to a teacher whose knowledge is easily communicated, as well as full and precise.

In this book the teacher's knowledge of his subject must be taken for granted. He will find in reality that however well-informed he may think himself, his knowledge, even of fairly elementary things, is incomplete for the purpose of teaching. If he is to keep alive and not merely to trade upon what he acquired before he began to teach, he will have constantly to be enlarging his knowledge of subjects and filling up gaps therein. Discipline has already been considered; but it must again be emphasised that method and discipline are dependent each on the other. The present chapter deals with method.

The word " method " is often used very loosely. One wrong use may be corrected at once. Method has been supposed to involve a body of fixed and stereotyped modes of procedure, each applicable to its appropriate subject as a kind of ritual to be observed by all teachers, and in all circumstances. Thus and thus must they set about a lesson on a poem, on simple interest, or on geographical contours. In this sense method has been rightly scorned and is now becoming discredited. No longer do we find that young teachers are expected to imitate model lessons as if they were patterns in a copybook, although such examples may be useful as illustrations of the general principles of method. But while it is true that good method is not merely a collection of artifices or mechanical devices and that every teacher must devise his own method, it is important to remember that good method can result only from the constant observation of certain broad principles. These include: orderly procedure in teaching, an arrangement of the subject matter which will avoid waste of time and of energy, and a distribution of emphasis which will secure the greatest co-operation from the pupils and maintain their active interest.

The older manuals of teaching used to advise young teachers to think of their lessons, and to write their preparatory notes on them under the heads Matter and Method, Method being used in the sense of a definite and stereotyped plan. Though the distinction was often pressed too far, and in the actual notes of lessons it was difficult to know what to put under one column and what under the other, the practice was not without value. For the two main principles of general method in teaching are the right selection and arrangement of the matter to be taught, and the right mode of bringing it to bear upon the class and of bringing the minds of the class to bear upon it. In the application of these principles will be found the basis of all good craftsmanship in teaching.

For the young teacher the " matter " of his teaching is usually already prescribed for him. It is not for him to decide whether his pupils should learn to read and draw, or should study history and geography, geometry or science. Even in details the path is often marked out ; usually he has to follow an arithmetic book which is provided for him and to use the reading books already in the class. In some schools and classes the heads and main topics in subjects like history, geography and science are laid down in a syllabus which the head master has drawn up. In other cases, the syllabus for an examination dictates the principal sub-divisions of a subject, even if it does no more than barely suggest the order in which they are to be taken.

The teacher is also bound to follow the general lines of treatment which the school as a whole adopts, whatever may be his private convictions as to their suitability and value. If the Direct Method of teaching a foreign language is used, he also must use it : if in history stress is laid in other classes, especially in those above his own, upon social or upon political history, he must adopt the same principle. There is no reason for the beginner to resent these restrictions. For in spite of them, and in spite of traditional and perhaps faulty methods which he may be required to adopt, the teacher, even the beginner, has a very wide liberty of choice and corresponding responsibility.

After all, it is he who selects the details of any lesson he gives, not forgetting the important factor of the language he himself uses in teaching. These cannot be imposed from without, nor will many head masters refuse a reasoned request of an assistant to vary the order of the major topics of a course which may have been set out in detail. For example, a teacher may be required to cover say thirty pages of a reading book within a certain period. It rests with him to determine whether he will go through the same number of pages each day (a foolish plan, usually, by the way) or go slowly at first and more quickly later, how many children he will call upon to read, which children and for how long, how much and how little he will explain, whether he will cover the ground rapidly and revise slowly, or the reverse, whether he will revise at all. So in arithmetic, if he is to teach the four rules as applied to easy fractions, he will himself have to decide when he will be at the blackboard and when he will set his class to work, when

E

and how he will deal with common mistakes, when and how he will help individual children, how far and by what means he will ask the class to make fractions themselves and experiment with them. In these examples selection of what to teach and the decision how to teach it are almost inextricably mingled. At the same time the teacher in his earlier years will do well to keep the " what " and the " how " separate in his mind when he is mapping out his course of teaching.

When he begins to arrange the course of teaching prescribed by the syllabus, the beginner, like other teachers, will do well to map out the stages of advance with care. Some writers have used the term " method-unit " to denote a portion of the main subject which can be treated as a complete whole. The name has a pedantic sound, but the idea of a unit of teaching is useful. It implies that certain facts can be grouped round one central idea, and related to it, so as to form an organised piece of knowledge. The important point to notice is that the unit of teaching is rarely the single lesson, confined to one period of a time-table. The single lesson is usually one step in a process, a step to be complete in itself and neatly rounded off, but to be regarded only as a link in a chain.

This is best explained by an illustration. Suppose that a term's work in geography for a young class is " Peoples of other Lands." The obvious main divisions will be the tropical, arctic and temperate lands and their inhabitants. These are too large to be units of teaching. The peoples of the tropics divide themselves, let us say, into those that inhabit the desert, the cultivated plains, the hot forests, the jungle. Each of these may be separated out as a unit of teaching, and the details under each of them duly prepared. Each requires more than one ordinary lesson period, of course ; what is needed is a series of lessons, each closely connected with what precedes and with what follows but the series constituting one whole. It is foolish to attempt to deal with peoples of the desert in one lesson period. For besides the opening description of the geographical features of a desert it will be necessary to describe life in tents, the oases, desert towns and villages, desert animals and plants, pasturage, caravans and transport. There must be time for pictorial illustrations to be properly seen and discussed. Most important of all the children must give back or reproduce in some fashion what they have learnt—by speech, by drawing, by written description, by the construction of a desert model in sand, or by several of these occupations. Revision must come in both at the end of each bit of teaching and to consolidate the whole.

The conception of building up a unit or a whole of teaching, with beginning, middle and end, will materially assist the teacher in selecting, not only the outstanding features of the instruction he is to convey, but also even the veriest details. He will be helped if he informs the class at the beginning what the subject is, and how long it will take to cover it ; pupils will often bring illustrative matter from home, and in any case a knowledge of the purpose and aim of the voyage of exploration will stimulate attention and confirm memory. The importance of the single lesson, apt to be over-estimated, diminishes when it is seen that it need not be a completed whole, in which everything necessary is exhausted. It should, of course, be as orderly in its way as the whole series, and the teacher should think out beforehand exactly what is to be said, done, shown or accomplished within the period. But unless it is the last of the series, it will be quite properly " continued in our next."

In arranging the subject matter, many teachers find the idea of " steps " or " sections " useful. A favourite formula was : Introduction, Presentation, Generalisation, and Application. These modes of contemplating a unit of teaching may no doubt be made too formal and pedantic, especially if the four steps are compressed within one lesson period. But " steps " often assist a beginner in plotting the distribution of the material at his disposal, though the process need not conform and in fact cannot always conform to a set model. The " application," that is the exercises by which the class carries out or applies what it has just learnt, does not always come at the end of a long preparatory period, but is made at each short step in the procedure. Many lessons need no " introduction " : " presentation " is an unsuitable term to use when the class is getting up something for itself, and " generalisation " is obviously out of place unless the subject lends itself to the elucidation of a general rule, principle or statement.

The young teacher should be warned against certain mistakes to which beginners are liable. The most serious of these is the tendency to overload each lesson period, particularly in lessons of the information kind, where the teacher is presenting to the class material almost wholly new to them. It is foolish to attempt in a science lesson to exhaust the topic of water or air within one period, or in a grammar lesson, to cover all that the children should know about subordinate clauses.

Allied to this mistake, and very often the cause of it, is the beginner's eagerness to tell his pupils all he knows himself. Fresh from an enthusiastic study of history or literature, he is apt to discharge upon his unfortunate pupils the contents of his own notebook on which the ink is scarcely dry. The selection of salient points, points which are important for the age of the children he is teaching, and the severe restriction of these to a few, are the marks of good teaching method. When once the appropriate main points are chosen, they may be embroidered by illustration, by vivid language, by being approached and led up to in varied ways. The class is to remember and apply the main features; if these are clearly expounded and emphasised aright, they will carry with them a great deal of subsidiary matter by natural association. If the young teacher acts on the advice given in the preceding paragraphs, and plots out his term's course, he will be in less danger of overweighting a particular lesson, and it is always useful for him to try to recall what he knew of the subject and how he regarded it when he was at the age of the pupils.

Another mistake of the beginner is to think that if he has successfully brought to a conclusion a good bit of teaching, his task is accomplished. His class have all understood the principle of a rule ; they have shown this by working some examples accurately and intelligently, and the teacher goes away elated, only to find by the next lesson that his efforts seem to have been almost wholly wasted, for the class has forgotten. There is nothing for it but patience and intelligently directed revision.

Revision, in mathematics especially, often means sheer repetition. In a series of lessons, it means a rapid recall at the beginning of what has been established in the preceding lessons. The need for this kind of recall must be kept in mind when a new lesson is planned. In grammar, for instance, the greater part of a new lesson may sometimes be usefully given to fresh examples and exercises on ground already covered, before the next step is attacked. In subjects such as reading, composition, and also in the elements of arithmetic, the " best method of revision is to go forward." In many schools a time is allowed for revision towards the end of term. This portion of the work needs as much careful planning as the more interesting earlier portions or it may degenerate into stale repetition without the verve and vigour of the first approach.

A further caution may be advanced. The teacher should beware of tedious and needless introductions to his lessons. It is of course his business, in opening up a new lesson, to bring to the surface the knowledge his class already possesses upon the matter in question. Sometimes a few rapid questions will effect the " recall " mentioned above. But very often a mere announcement of the subject will serve as well : it will certainly be better than a wearisome attempt by " eliciting " miscellaneous information from the class, to bring their minds to bear upon the subject. " Page so and so " is an adequate introduction to an ordinary reading lesson ; " to-day we get on to the multiplication of decimals " will serve to begin one on arithmetic ; " our business to-day is to start on the geography of India " will launch a geography lesson.

CHAPTER VII

GENERAL PRINCIPLES OF TEACHING—II

THE foregoing chapter deals principally with the selection and arrangement of the matter to be taught, though it also includes some consideration of method. There are other aspects of method which should now receive attention.

Let us contrast two types of teaching which have had their vogue. In one the pupil prepares a lesson at home, writes an exercise, learns some grammar, prepares a piece of translation, gets up a chapter in history, answers questions or does a map in geography, works a series of sums. The work is shown up and corrected, or the lesson is heard next day. The teacher limits himself to correcting errors, reproving the inaccurate and indolent ; he seldom gives a systematic lesson, though he does incidentally explain or enunciate a rule. He talks very little except to ask questions or correct mistakes. If any time is left over the class is set to work to learn or to write something else.

In the other type of teaching the class comes in with no preparation at all. The teacher assumes them to be completely ignorant of his theme and he proceeds to develop it with a great deal of talking on his own part and very little, save in answer to questions, on theirs ; sometimes also with a large expenditure of chalk.

These are, of course, extremes, with obvious and glaring defects. In one the teacher does little except examine ; in the other the class does little except listen. But the first has the great merit of making really serious demands on the class, by the exercises they do and the questions they answer or fail to answer, and it carries the advantage of informing the teacher how they are progressing. The pupils learn to work by and for themselves and to use books. Their errors are severely dealt with, at any rate by word of mouth, and insensibly they begin to know the difference between trifling mistakes, slips that are pardonable, and gross mistakes, likely to be visited with the utmost wrath. Teaching of the second type affords a great opening to the able teacher. By a judicious combination of continued exposition and skilful questioning he can carry a class with him, and lead them to see and appreciate what they could not grasp alone. He can replace the dry text book in history or geography by vivid description, and inspire a respect, and even a liking, for literature by his own rendering of it. He can play upon his class as on an instrument, and utilise to the full the advantages of the living voice.

The best teaching will avoid the defects of these extreme methods while displaying their advantages. It will give the class work to do, and yet will not degenerate into the mere examining of work done. It will mean talking and talking plentifully in the right place, but without any haranguing. It would not be an exaggeration to say that good method, in the sense we are now considering, consists in the teacher knowing when he should talk to teach and when he should set his class to learn by themselves.

The beginner need not be unduly disturbed by the suggestion that his lessons are " talk and chalk," and that his pupils are mere listeners. As we have constantly reiterated in these pages, pupils should be doers. But after all young children do acquire a great deal of their knowledge of the world by listening, and to a large degree they come to school to listen. Listening has been the mode of getting inspiration and knowledge from the time of the prophets, and all the mass of print in the world has not yet done away with this primitive and fundamentally sound way of learning. But in a good class the listening need not be passive, for it may and should lead to activity, and the pupils should be stimulated by it to do something themselves, if only to repeat in their own way what they have heard and apprehended. Listening does not always imply a monologue by one speaker, though now and then, as with a story, the uninterrupted monologue is perfectly in place. The teacher must preserve a balance.

Broadly regarded, the talking lesson will count for more with younger children than with older. In her anxiety to let young children teach themselves, Madame Montessori has been apt to overlook the natural liking of children for listening, and being instructed by word of mouth. When for a time, they have been busily and happily engaged with apparatus, teaching themselves to read, working little sums, making or drawing something or engaged in other occupations, children will gladly flock round the teacher and sit absorbed listening with all their ears to a story or to an interesting chat.

So also at a much later age, when a class of boys or girls have been hunting up matter in their history books, or collecting information in geography, or puzzling over a chapter in everyday science, or again have been working sums, or writing vigorously, or drawing, they will welcome with relief even a continuous " lecture " from the teacher who gathers up the threads, clears away difficulties, adds vivid illustrations, opens out new vistas, or shows how all the facts can be linked together into a rational and intelligible whole of knowledge. Once more the place of talk, as well as the place of chalk, is just one of those points of method or technique which the youngest teacher must carefully consider, and, subject to advice from older people, determine ultimately for himself.

If talking is of such importance as one of the principal tools of the teacher, the medium by which it is conveyed, the English tongue in England, requires careful attention. Reference is made elsewhere to the question of " standard " English, the native tongue accurately delivered and clearly and correctly pronounced. The teacher must speak in the way in which he would wish his pupils to speak, as to both distinctness and exactitude. He need not be prim, still less need he be bookish ; he can be forceful and idiomatic without falling into slang.

On the other hand there is a distinct danger that he may be simple to babyishness. In a large degree it is from him that the class will pick up the use of new and unfamiliar words and expressions in spoken English. Accordingly, if he can gauge it right, no easy business, his language should be a little beyond that which would exactly suit the level of the class. Examples are open to obvious criticism, but one may be risked. English contains a very large number of " doublets," words and phrases coming from the older elements of the language and words and phrases of more recent " learned " origin ; " soon " and " immediately " —" join together " and " connect "—" strong " and " vigorous "—are examples. The teacher may deliberately at the right time prefer the more " learned " word. The class will have the vague ideas gathered from their reading clarified by hearing the words used in an unmistakable way ; needless to say, the teacher should not " explain " the words at this point.

Allied to this delicate question is that of technical terms. Some persons try to avoid them with young children, under the impression that they are " hard." They speak of " name-words " instead of " nouns," and shy at petals and stamens when speaking of flowers. It is true that these terms may be ludicrously over-emphasised, as when in an old form of object lesson, a long catalogue of adjectives, soluble, transparent, porous, opaque, ductile, malleable, and the like, was brought in to describe the properties of a mineral. But, judiciously chosen and sparingly introduced, technical terms are not only useful but attractive. Witness the eagerness with which children, boys especially, acquire the technical terms belonging to motors, railways and wireless. The special language of geography, when properly introduced, has offered no real difficulty in the past ; in science very often only technical terms possess the required exactness. In history, where the special words, like conquest, law, invasion, parliament, empire, dominion, are more abstract, the difficulty is of course much greater. This must be faced and misconceptions gradually corrected as they reveal themselves. It may be noted in passing that the delight of children in technical terms is due to the sense of power in being able to use them. This fact offers a valuable hint to the teacher.

The older method books give a good deal of attention to the art of questioning, and the related art of dealing with answers, especially with imperfect answers. They were right, for clever questioning is a mark of high skill. It cannot be taught by mere rules, though the directions usually given are certainly not to be despised. Questions should be unmistakably clear, economical in phrasing, relevant to the point to be brought out. Vague questions are as bad as vague commands, and as fatal to good discipline in their own way. This is obvious common sense : to ignore it is to waste time.

It is also sometimes advised that questions should not suggest the answers, and that they should not admit of being answered in one word. That depends. The teacher may deliberately frame his question to give a lead as to the answer, for it may suit his purpose to do so. The unwary teacher sometimes suggests the answer inadvertently by the form of the question, or the emphasis with which he asks it. Some children are extremely clever to detect what answer the teacher hopes for, and to give that instead of their real belief or opinion. The second suggestion is palpably absurd, and is parallel to the rule which has been known to be imposed, that children should answer in complete sentences. Very many questions require one word and one word only. What are 4 × 15 ? Who was the prelate with whom Henry II quarrelled ? Others are quite properly met by a phrase. Others require a clear statement of some length. The teacher should know what he wants, and frame his question accordingly.

More important than directions as to the form of question and of answer is a consideration of the purpose of questioning, and the various occasions and objects of questioning. The idea of questioning at all is, of course, sound enough ; it is one of the easiest and best ways of ensuring the co-operation of the class. The occasions for questioning vary, and with them the type of questions may vary accordingly.

The simplest occasion which may, as it were, be separated out, is the examination, when the teacher wishes to discover whether his class has a firm and accurate grasp of certain information, the multiplication table, the spelling of certain words, the facts of geography and history, dates, formulæ, declensions and conjugations, and meanings of words in Latin and French. This kind of questioning occurs in formal oral or written examination at the end of term, or in revision when a particular piece of work has been covered, in a summary at the end of a bit of teaching, in the testing of work done during preparation—all occasions when the aim is to ascertain chiefly the knowledge of facts. Questions here should be very definite and brief, and few comments on the answers are necessary. Of course all examination questions are not of the terse type now suggested, for they may require considered and thoughtful answers, and have to be framed with care in order to be clear and "fool-proof." But, in contrast with other forms of questioning, the examination kinds can usefully be kept apart in the teacher's mind.

The other forms are sometimes classed together as "teaching" questions. Without emphasising the label too much, for all questions should subserve the ends of teaching, it may be said that these are rather single questions or series of questions occurring in a lesson and, therefore, intended to make the pupil do some active thinking on his own account, and not merely to recall information. "Teaching" questions are in place when teacher and class are pursuing a connected piece of reasoning or argument, e.g. in the demonstration of a rule in arithmetic or the elucidation of a principle in science or geography when one question follows the answer to another in a sort of Socratic dialogue.

Apart from sustained argument, " teaching " questions occur sporadically everywhere, just as the other kind do. The teacher should of set purpose occasionally compose questions with the definite intention, not of examining, but of clarifying impressions and removing misconceptions. The young teacher would do well to invent imaginary dialogues in which these questions would come, planning in grammar for example how he would bring out the idea of the passive or the function of the adjective. The exercise will be salutary, even if the actual course of the lesson does not precisely follow the imagined preliminary sketch. If he is fortunate enough to be able to listen to an experienced teacher at work, he should note what questions evoke the best answers, and frankly appropriate them for his own use.

The two types of question described are useful to distinguish, but the distinction must not be pressed too far, as if every occasion for questioning were bound to conform to one or the other. The instrument of questioning must be flexible and serviceable on all occasions, foreseen and unforeseen. What is to be guarded against is an incessant rain of questions poured out on to the class under the wrong impression that this is teaching ; and also against asking information questions with the idea that consecutive and logical reasoning is being cultivated. The teacher should decide beforehand —or on the spur of the moment—how much in a talking lesson he will hold forth himself and how much obtain by questioning ; when he will interrupt a discourse by questions, and when stop a series of questions and take the floor himself. So when he meets with difficult words in a reading lesson he must determine when he will seek to " elicit " the meaning by questioning the class, and when he will merely tell it and pass on. For example the meaning of a word like " obnoxious " may be won from an intelligent class, if the teacher gives other examples of its use ; the meaning of new words like " pirogue " or " glacier " must be told outright.

A few other pieces of general advice may be offered on questioning. Young teachers should address questions to individuals and not to the whole class. They should at first avoid questions like " does anyone know ? " until they are in full command of the class. Otherwise answering is apt to be sporadic and even simultaneous, control goes and time is wasted. This advice is cautionary ; for a skilled teacher can do many things and permit many things which a novice cannot, though in the matter of questioning classes and individuals even experienced teachers often waste much time.

Young teachers are also told not to repeat answers. Nothing in fact is more dreary than to listen to a set of questions and answers, with every answer repeated by the teacher. The pupil must answer in a way to be heard by all the class and if so,

F

repetition is both useless and tedious. So the advice is good, especially at first. It may, however, be necessary to repeat an answer for emphasis, as, for example, in a continued course of reasoning, giving the class time to appreciate what is said and what it really means. It is the echo repetition that is to be avoided, and no teaching vice is more insidious in its onset or more difficult for the victim to eradicate.

A teacher's skill and resource are shown in a high degree by his way of dealing with answers. There are no rules. It is unwise to pass over all wrong answers, as it is unwise to attempt to deal with all ; some are genuine misconceptions which the teacher must clear up at the time or later on, others are imperfect and incomplete answers, genuine also, which must be rounded off, others are haphazard or stupid and should be treated with contempt or else with such brief but emphatic words of disapproval as the teacher may have at command. A consistently bad set of answers means that the lesson itself is somehow wrong ; above the level of the class at the time, or at any rate unskilfully presented.

We may also utter a passing protest against receiving answer after answer with the same phrase of commendation. Often no phrase is required and always the teacher should avoid a mechanical repetition of such words as " Yes, that's right ! " or " All right," or " Very good," etc.

In what is said above, it is assumed that the questioner is the teacher. Why not the class ?

The practised teacher will no doubt not only allow but encourage questions from his class ; in some kinds of lesson, questions will occur as naturally as in conversation, on both sides. But the beginner should for a while be cautious in inviting questions from the class. They will come too freely, they will often be quite irrelevant, and it is beyond his skill at first to cope with a shower of questions. Let questions arise by all means, but until the novice can, at a word, calm down exuberance, he will be wise to do nothing to excite it. Perhaps the best occasion is a reading lesson, where pupils ought to say what words, phrases or allusions they do not understand. So also at the end of a bit of teaching in mathematics or geography or science, the teacher may well invite questions on points which have not been understood by all. When he can get on such terms with his class that they will frankly say when they are puzzled, instead of dumbly acquiescing and professing to understand when they do not, a beginner is on the way to becoming a good teacher.

Some reference should be made in a chapter upon method to those principles of teaching to which Herbert Spencer gave so prominent a place in his famous book on Education. " Proceed," said he, " from simple to complex, from known to unknown, from particular to general, from concrete to abstract." The general trend of these axioms is clearly the same : they are exemplifications of the procedure from simple to less simple. As general rules they are unexceptionable. But they are not always easy to apply to details of practice.

All subjects do not develop from simple elements with the orderly precision of Euclid, and if they did, the mind of the pupil does not grow alongside in the same way. So " simple " must not be construed as if it could be applied only and always to the logical ultimate foundations of a subject as seen by a philosophic expert. " Simple," like " known," is relative to the mind of the pupil. Children make jumps and learn for the most part in an order which is far from logical and far from regular. They will joyfully count by tens to the triumphant " one hundred " when their acquaintance with numbers like thirteen and seventeen is of the most meagre. They will rejoice to hear of adventures in the desert when they have never seen a piece of wild nature, still less a stretch of barren sand. Though innocent of any knowledge of internal combustion they will eagerly become proficient in the working gadgets of a motor-car. They have an infinite capacity for taking the complex and unknown for granted. The teacher will often find it a great advantage to plunge straight into the unknown and work back, and at times to begin even in mathematics with the complex. But of course, broadly speaking the maxims, simple to complex, known to related unknown, are true. Only they need common sense in the carrying out.

The other two principles, particular to general, concrete to abstract, are of less use. Teaching is by no means all, or even mainly, a procedure from particulars to establish a general rule. In some subjects, like history, the less of the "general" there is, the better in the earlier stages. The general rules of reading, spelling and grammar have mainly to be taught dogmatically, and not approached through particulars as if the pupils were receiving a premature training in scientific method. They have not to be proved ; they are laws almost in the legal sense, not uniformities of nature in the scientific sense, and they need asserting and not establishing. All this does not mean that particular examples are not essential, but they are essential to support and exemplify and not to "proceed to the general."

The difficulty of applying the axiom "from concrete to abstract" is to decide precisely which is which. How does one select the "concrete" in early lessons on stocks and shares ? What is concrete and what abstract in discussing the climate of the monsoon regions ? In early arithmetic, it is true, the actual measurements by pacing and ruling, handling and weighing, by the use of a clock face, should precede the abstract rules ; and these methods may be properly called concrete. But the word is often much misused and, to be plain, the teacher may, without harm, forget this particular phrase as an application of the sound principle of advancing from what is known and simple to the pupil to what is less known and less simple.

The general directions on method in teaching which have been given in this and the last chapter may be summed up in one word : "technique."

Technique is not everything in teaching. Looked at from an ideal point of view it is not the most important element in teaching at its highest. But for want of it much good teaching, otherwise well conceived, fails of its effect. It is of importance to the beginner, not only because it helps him to become a good craftsman, which he must become if he is to be a good teacher, but also because it is a strong support to him in his early experimental years. In its essentials it is no difficult art to be painfully acquired by a long apprenticeship since the beginner can practise it from the very first.

There is nothing mystical about technique. It is just intelligent procedure which saves teacher and class both time and energy and keeps the teaching clear and intelligible. Some of the larger constituents of technique, the proper selection of material, and the clear laying out of the lessons, the right use of language, have been fully discussed. There is technique also in matters apparently indifferent, the actual arrangement of the class so that they can see and be seen, hear and be heard, in the right use of the blackboard, in the effortless and matter of fact distribution of tasks to be done, even in the passing of books and materials and their collection. Precision and ease in the mechanics of teaching go a long way towards securing and maintaining control. Technique in these matters leads to workmanlike teaching, in which teacher and pupils feel that they are getting on.

Technique can, of course, be abused. It can be turned into a smart, hard and metallic kind of intercourse between teacher and class, which, if brilliant, is soulless and in the long run is wearying to all concerned. A teacher with good technique and nothing beyond may be little more than an instruction-monger. At bottom it is a series of good habits, flexible, not rigid, neither a ritual nor a series of rules. The good habits should be begun from the very first. As the young teacher grows in experience his technique will become less obvious and less mechanical. It will, in fact, develop into style, and in teaching, as in literature, style is the expression of a man's personality.

CHAPTER VIII

THE STAGES IN EDUCATION

As this book is primarily an introduction to principles and methods of teaching, it cannot pretend to review the modes of treating all subjects commonly taught in schools. It can only indicate the nature of the problems that arise, offer certain suggestions for the guidance of young teachers and refer them to other sources of information.

In an appendix will be found an annotated list of suitable books. Among these special attention may be drawn to the *Suggestions for the Consideration of Teachers and Others*, issued by the Board of Education at the cost of 2*s*. The latest edition should be consulted. The " Suggestions " are intended for elementary schools in the first instance, and they do not touch upon subjects, such as foreign languages, which are not usually taught in these schools. But the range of subjects in elementary schools is so wide, and the common ground in all forms of education up to the age of fifteen is so extensive that what is said applies for the most part without any modification to the education of all children up to the age named. The book, as its title indicates, is one of suggestions founded upon observation of the best methods now current. They are suggestions only and not regulations or prescriptions. Naturally it is schools with classes of substantial size that are mainly considered ; but teachers of small classes and of individual children, in private schools as well as in schools under public authorities, will find much that is of positive value to them.

Before dealing with the teaching of subjects under separate headings, some general observations must be made upon stages in education. It is becoming customary to think of school life as divisible into two main periods, primary, and secondary or post-primary. The best educational opinion favours a division at about eleven years of age. This age, it is believed, marks the end of a stage in physical and in mental growth, and, broadly speaking, the characteristics of the years following can be distinguished from those of the years preceding with more certainty than they can at earlier periods of development. Below eleven the child retains some relics of infancy ; above it, he shows signs of approaching adolescence and maturity.

More important than a precise delimitation by age, however, is the conception of the primary period as that in which a child should acquire the tools of learning. He should be taught to read, write, draw, calculate and to use his hands and fingers, and taught all these in a systematic way. He should also have been introduced to the elements of a body of knowledge which will become the basis for further instruction in subjects such as geography, history, science, beyond the primary stage. What this summary definition may mean in detail will appear in due course. It is to be noted that the primary stage has not in the past corresponded in fact very closely with the usual forms of school organisation, though there are signs that a closer correspondence may be made in the future. The Preparatory School goes beyond it ; so does the ordinary elementary school, while the Infants' School and the Kindergarten do not fill it. From the point of view of these chapters, in which we discuss how the separate constituents of primary education can be taught, the want of correspondence between theory and actual organisation is of little consequence.

The primary stage can be further divided with advantage for our present purpose. It is one of the peculiarities of English education—one may go farther, and say one of its glories—that the English have given much thought and trouble to the education of very young children. The inspiration came largely, no doubt, from abroad, from Froebel and from American writers, and, much later, from Mme. Montessori, but special attention to this period of a child's education derives from Engish practice. The Kindergarten and the Infants' School are its manifestations. A special technique for teaching young children has developed here and in the United States, and, in more recent years, in Italy.

Accordingly it is necessary, as well as useful, to discuss separately the teaching of the youngest children. No very precise age limit can be assigned to the period when pupils are to be considered to be young children. Roughly speaking, the special methods appropriate to them should become merged in methods more suitable for children less young by the time the children are eight. By this age, and often earlier, the pupil is a " boy " or " girl " and not a " child," whose sex is unimportant. Even in some well-to-do homes, where formal instruction under a governess may begin as late as 7 or 8, the methods of teaching should be more robust than those tenderer methods which are appropriate to children below those ages. The Nursery School cannot be considered here. The suggestions which follow are for teachers in schools of the usual types, public and private, and for teachers of young children at home.

In this first period of the primary stage the school education of the child is to begin. This is to be distinguished from the education he has been receiving and will continue to receive outside the schoolroom. He will in most cases be introduced to a new society, and everywhere to some kind of systematic instruction. The aim of the instruction is to enlarge his knowledge of the world he lives in, and to increase his capacity for dealing with it ; the means are his association with teacher and companions, the language they use, the activities in which they are all engaged. He is also to break ground in reading, writing (with drawing) and number, the arts which lie at the roots of education at the present time. Viewed from another angle, the school is to foster and direct into right channels those appetites, curiosities and eager interests to which reference has been made in an earlier chapter ; to feed the growing mind and watch over and train the developing body.

Children have already learnt an enormous amount in the few years before coming to school. They are to continue the process under expert guidance, and not to have something wholly uncongenial forced upon them. They are gradually to be trained upon a regular plan, and yet are to retain the freshness and even some of the incidental and casual characteristics of the modes in which they have already won the knowledge they possess. Though they are in schools or schoolrooms they are not suddenly to be condemned to immobility, but, so far as possible, to have plenty of freedom of movement. In so far as schoolroom conditions permit, they are to feel as much at ease in the classroom as in their own homes. With all this freedom they are to learn the necessary discipline of community life, and gradually to be introduced to the discipline of learning. The function of the teacher, viewed in this light, is one which calls for all the intelligence and sympathy, the common sense as well as the patience and tenderness, that the teacher can command.

The teaching of these young children has undergone a complete revolution in the last fifty years. The note of the old instruction, in almost all schools, was drill, and class drill at that for the most part. The children sat in uniform rows for longer periods than they would do if they were left free, did not speak unless they were required to do so, and then very often spoke in chorus. They learnt the alphabet by drill, naming the letters but not for some time combining them in words, spelled aloud, read simultaneously, chanted the multiplication table, and wrote from copies, but never wrote what they would like to write. Drill even governed their handwork: Froebel's "gifts" were touched, moved, arranged and put aside to the word of command. There was no room for spontaneity or the assertion of individual tastes.

Strange to say, the children did learn by this method, and under an amiable and skilful teacher enjoyed it. There was a sort of exhilaration in a noisy class chorus. Children, who at home were restless and mischievous, accepted the discipline ; it provided them with an unceasing occupation, and one which a clever teacher never made unduly tiring. Harassed mothers, unskilled in the art of keeping their children going at home, perpetually wondered how their turbulent and uneasy boys and girls were induced by the teachers to become model children in the Infants' School.

The method had obvious defects. The restraint imposed was, in reality, unnatural. The individual was submerged in the class. Those who were, in a school sense, bright and intelligent, made progress enough, and their native zest and resourcefulness were not damped by what, on the surface, was deadening routine. But those who, again in a school sense, were slow and dull, often merely followed the leaders in a chorus, and themselves learnt slowly and unintelligently, while such powers of application and of self-help as they possessed were undeveloped.

The best teachers nowadays advocate methods which are called " individual methods." Restraint is reduced to a minimum, and school furniture is now chosen which will not condemn the children to sitting still more than is necessary. Classes are often broken up into groups, and, more important, each child is given apparatus that for the time being is his own. Material, such as letters and syllables on cards, is supplied to the children that they may be able to make words themselves ; counters of all kinds are distributed so that the children can learn number by experiment, and by handling things that can be counted ; each child has his own writing and drawing material. Where the furniture of the room permits, each child fetches his own boxes and puts them away. The teacher moves round the class, directing, assisting and suggesting.

The extreme form of the individual method is that which is advocated by Mme. Montessori, in which, with the help of ingenious but simple devices, the pupil teaches himself to read, to write, and to count, and learns to discriminate between shapes and sizes, colours and weights, thus training his senses without substantial interference from the teacher, and wholly without any regard to the needs of other members of a class.

Before the doctrines of Mme. Montessori had reached England, English teachers of young children had begun to break down the domination of the class idea. The best of them had long abandoned the worst forms of class drill and chorus work, and had adopted methods of teaching the subjects which necessarily called for more attention to individuals, especially in handwork and what were called " Kindergarten Occupations." The idea of setting children to make their own reading and their own sums came a little later, and it has been carried out in various ways, for here the teacher is bound by no rigid method, and has full scope for ingenuity and inventiveness.

What has just been said must not be interpreted as meaning that there are two diametrically opposed methods which are alternative. Indeed a danger lies here to which an enthusiastic teacher may be exposed. For the ordinary class, small or large, as seen in schools, class teaching is not less important than the teaching on an individual method. In reading, writing and number the class requires to be gathered together for the demonstration of some fresh step or for revision, and at times for the simple pleasure and value of a good class lesson. A large part of the work of a teacher of young children must be talks with the whole class, as in the telling of stories, or in the early lessons on familiar things. Obviously also, concerted activity in music and physical exercises with dancing imply a class taken as a whole. No small demand is made on a teacher's good sense, when she decides the occasions for class work and for individual work. No one who has seen the satisfaction and eager anticipation with which a number of children, busily engaged for some time in work by themselves, settle down as a class to hear a story or have a talk can doubt that collective instruction is an essential element of good teaching method at this stage.

The distinction we have made between two portions of the primary stage, the earlier and the later, should not lead the unwary into supposing that there should be a decided break in continuity between them, either in methods or in discipline. The freedom and spontaneity of the children in the Infants' and Kindergarten classes can be preserved in classes beyond, and something of the system and precision applicable to children who are approaching eleven should be introduced at a much earlier period.

A piece of advice which is generally applicable to teachers of all classes and grades is especially in place at the transition from the first years of the primary stage to the later years. Even if children are not actually transferred to another department or school and there is no definite break, it is well to bear the advice in mind. Where there is a break, as between Infants' School and Senior School, Kindergarten and Lower Forms, it is all important. The teacher should find out, and know accurately, what his pupils have done in the previous class.

The neglect of this obvious piece of common sense has produced perhaps more bad teaching and irritation than any other common failing in teachers, and especially in teachers of the lowest classes in elementary schools and earlier forms in secondary schools. Fresh from the completion of a year's work with their class they are apt to expect that the newcomers have been taught on similar lines, and attained a similar kind of standard. When they make a preliminary test they apply the criteria suitable to their own class, and very often they fail to discover the real acquisitions and the real powers of children who have been under a different type of teaching. It is emphatically their business to discover the best results of the earlier teaching and to make use of them. Few classes that come up even from a good Kindergarten or an Infants' School are uniform in attainments, as measured by the power to read, spell and do certain sums. But they should be uniform in having power to attack new work and a zest in doing so. There need be no violent break between the methods of the Kindergarten and those of the classes above it.

The methods appropriate to the later years of the primary stage naturally differ in some important respects from those which characterise a good Infants' School or Kindergarten. The courses of instruction are laid down with more precision, and it is expected that a certain amount of ground will be covered in a certain time. Even if the standards of the old Codes for Elementary Schools are not imposed, the work is in some degree standardised. Accordingly the teaching is no longer incidental in appearance, and the demands made on the children call for more systematic effort sustained for longer periods. The powers of the children are growing, and they are ready to respond to a more robust kind of teaching. The curiosity and receptivity of the early years remain and should not be impaired by clumsy handling. But they can now be directed into more orderly channels.

By common consent, it is agreed that during the years from about seven or eight up to the end of the primary stage and a little beyond children can absorb fresh knowledge with ease, if it is properly presented. They are not fastidious, but they will not retain permanently what does not engage their interest. This interest, however, is not the interest of a mature and trained mind establishing the connections between various parts of a subject or different subjects. It is the interest of simple acquirement, and it may be evoked in lessons primarily directed towards such exercises as the learning of tables, declensions, etc.

The individual methods we have mentioned now give place to more formal class instruction, with its special advantages and dangers. The teacher must not forget the individual in the class, but usually he has fewer opportunities of permitting the members of his class to proceed at their own rate and by their own efforts. It is true that on such plans as the Dalton plan individual pupils work by and for themselves. But in the pages that follow we have assumed that above the Infants' stage children are taught for the most part in classes according to the prevailing custom. For the majority of teachers the craft of teaching has to do with classes. The method must be systematic without degenerating into drill, and teachers have a complex task in conducting a whole class without destroying the individual activity of its members.

Although this book does not deal with the stages beyond the primary, we may note that the post-primary stage assumes that those who enter upon it already possess the tools of learning, which they have exercised in the various subjects that constitute primary education. This stage is the bridge between boyhood and girlhood on the one hand, with their necessary concomitants, guidance and discipline, and, on the other hand, the independence and self-reliance of maturity. Instruction during the post-primary years, whether gained in a Secondary School or in any other school, should make the pupil ready and able to extend his interest and knowledge into ever-widening fields. What he ultimately becomes and what directions his interest will take, are determined very largely by his surroundings, by his means of gaining a livelihood and by the social and political ideals of the community to which he belongs. These external influences will necessarily be powerful, but in an educated person there should be a constant development of individuality. The grown man or woman will then be something more than a mere unit in commerce and industry. Their education, begun under guidance, and continued under impulsion from within themselves, should confirm in them the possession of inner sources of satisfaction such as will be obtained only from the efficient exercise of their own powers in all that they undertake, whether in the way of business or of leisure.

CHAPTER IX

THE CURRICULUM : THE MOTHER TONGUE

THE elements of learning which should form the staple of early instruction have been held by tradition to be reading, writing and arithmetic. Modern writers on education would hardly accept the tradition of the " Three R's " in its bare form. For the first, reading, they would substitute the mother tongue, which will embrace speech, reading and composition. They would consider writing as one aspect of drawing, and both as examples of practical and manual activity to be developed from the beginning. Arithmetic, understood as something more than simple computation, would be retained. But, though interpreted in a wider sense, the three R's still remain as the implements of instruction. To teach them and to have them practised on suitable material is still the main business of the primary stage ; and it is as important as ever to lay sound foundations.

The teaching of the mother tongue may be conveniently considered under several heads, of which speech, reading and composition will be the chief. Though there may be differences in the methods of treating each in the introductory stages and in the later years, it is to be borne in mind that the subjects themselves are one throughout.

Speech.

The importance of speech does not call for demonstration. With young children, speech permeates all lessons, and if it be true that " every teacher is a teacher of English " in schools for older children, it is just as true in schools for the youngest. The young teacher can usefully distinguish several aspects of speech. Her own speech should be above reproach, accurate and not slipshod, clear and pleasant to listen to, in simple but not babyish English, varied in vocabulary, vivid in phrase, terse at times and full at other times, a pattern which the children may properly imitate.

The speech of the pupils will need both correction and amplification. Amplification must be left to be a general result of the whole of the teaching. Correction offers difficulties, and here the teacher should discriminate. Speech which is incorrect in a grammatical sense should not be too assiduously noticed with young children. Here and there a child, who is telling or re-telling a story or answering a question, may be reminded that we say " horses are " and not " horses is," and that " those things " sounds better than " them things." But the grammatically correct phrase need not be a matter of grave concern at this stage. On the other hand the teacher should give careful attention to " speech defects." She should have enough knowledge of phonetics, or of how English sounds are produced by a good speaker, to detect improper sounds. The commonest defects are in the pronunciation of th (given as f or v) and s (given as a lisp) ; but some children have difficulty with n l t (and d) c or k (and g). The dropping of the " h " is not strictly a speech defect. Children with the real defects should be taken aside, if a casual correction in class is not enough, and given a little private drill. It is very desirable, as early as possible, to remove the handicap that a defect in speech brings. For information how to deal with defects the books named in the Appendix should be consulted.

But the problem of speech is more than the correction of defects of the kind mentioned. It is that of training the children to speak freely and naturally. There is no royal road to this end. The teacher, young or old, should keep it in view in all lessons, encouraging the shy and helping the inarticulate. No set lessons on " speech " as such are necessary. All the story-telling lessons and the miscellaneous talks, ranging from general conversation on the seasons, on plants, animals and birds, to the more systematically planned discussions leading up to simple geographical notions, should be used to make individual children speak ; they may not only answer questions, but re-tell stories, act them with dialogue, learn and recite simple verses and play games which call for speaking.

The teaching of the three R's, whether collectively or individually, will also afford ample opportunity for encouraging clear and correct utterance, with free expression of the children's own thoughts. Children chatter in ordinary cases at home or at play. Once it would have been thought a dangerous heresy to suggest they should talk in school. Yet it is largely by conversation with others that children have learnt what they have learnt before coming to school, and the process should be continued in this early stage so far as circumstances allow. The fact that there are so many in one class who must all have a chance of speaking will effectively prevent undue loquacity in the few. Talkativeness in itself is not the aim, but the natural responsiveness of an un-selfconscious child.

As the children advance up the school the question of correct speech assumes a greater importance than in the earlier years. Systematic endeavour to train children in speaking their native tongue correctly is clearly necessary, but the extent of the teacher's responsibility and the means by which he can carry it out are not self-evident. Correct English may be understood in two senses, first, the accurate use of good English in speaking and writing, free from grammatical blunders, slang and solecisms, and second, clear articulation and a pronunciation which at any rate approaches standard English.

To treat pronunciation first, the difficulties in securing good pronunciation vary very widely in schools. In many, where children have learnt to speak a kind of standard English at home, the chief preoccupation of the teacher will be to correct occasional defects of speech, and positive errors, and as new words arise, to give the correct quantity and accentuation—relatively an easy task. But in most schools the troublesome question of local pronunciation arises, and even where dialect in a narrow sense is not implicated, there are common mispronunciations.

Where classes are large, the teacher can do little beyond setting a good example, and making occasional corrections. Two or three suggestions, however, may be made. In the first place in pronunciation, and it may be added, in respect of many grammatical mistakes, the distinction should not be between right and wrong English but between good English and English that is not good. The absence of " h " where it is usually sounded should not be called wrong English : it is not good or the best current English. The vowel " u " as pronounced north of the Trent, and the Cockney diphthongs which represent " a " and " o " are not wrong but just not the best. It is absurd to say that they are not English when they are habitually used by some millions of English people. In many parts of the country it is no use whatever trying to substitute in its entirety a supposed " standard " English very remote from the local form.

Experts tell us that the aim should be to reach a " regional " standard English pronunciation, which, though it may betray the local origin, is comprehensible outside the region. It is mainly an affair of vowels and diphthongs, although not exclusively so. The regional standard in the North, for example, will have in words like " but," " rub,"

" trouble," a " u " midway, as it were, between the local " u," which usually is like the " u " in " put " and " pull," and the " u " of the Southerner. So the Southern pronunciation of " a " in " came," rather like " kah-eem," will be modified. How far it is possible to soften the peculiarities of the dialect in some places may be a matter of opinion. If an attempt is made, it should be in the direction indicated.

The second suggestion is that the teacher would do wisely to confine his efforts to what may be called " public " speech when seeking to standardise pronunciation and to amend speech in general in regard to grammar and distinctness. He should always expect a high standard (suitable to the locality), when the pupil is reading aloud, is reciting, is answering questions and asking them, is in fact " on parade " in school. But speech out of school, pronunciation and all, must be left to fortune. It was noticed in the War that private soldiers assumed a form of polite speech to their officers, while they talked among themselves in dialect and in slang.

This suggestion amounts to an advocacy of bi-lingualism. Why not ? Speech is useless if it is not easily understood by the hearer, and the extreme forms of English dialect are unintelligible to an Englishman from another county. To have two kinds of speech, one for " public " use, for Sundays, as it were, and another for one's intimates, is a sign of education rather than of the want of it. Most people probably are bi-lingual, at least in the sense that they speak with more care and force when they are to be heard by a company than when in their own private circle.

The third suggestion also bears upon the " public " speech here suggested. It is more important that speech should be vigorous and clear than that pronunciation should be accurate. Slurring and elision of consonants, the dropping of some short syllables, the deadening of some vowels which with speakers of acknowledged merit have a clear sound of their own, all these make speech slipshod and therefore obscure. These defects, and they are defects from the point of view of clear speech, are found in all classes of society and are not peculiar to those who speak dialect ; in fact many dialects are quite remarkably crisp and distinct. There is no need for pedantry here. In " public speech," " all right " need not be absurdly pronounced " all-ll right-tt " in order to avoid the cockney " aw-eye."

A further suggestion may be permitted. In schools, such as are here considered, mainly elementary schools, some local peculiarities may be left alone, the peculiar " r " of the Tyne and of the West, for example. Schools which are fortunately situated, secondary schools, and some suburban elementary schools, can no doubt go further in the direction of cultivated English ; their danger is less the prevalence of violent local forms than that of lazily pronounced and slipshod speech. In aiming at good speech, the teacher will have to be discreet. He should not fritter away his time by

constant and nagging correction of errors. Dramatic
work and the practice of oral composition should
help him considerably, especially the former ; the
children will see the need for accuracy when they
are to speak a part, and they will lose some of that
self-consciousness which hampers correct speech in
their ordinary surroundings. The teacher should
not scorn even what seem to him to be ugly dialect
forms. He must beware of being too positive, for
English pronunciation varies in good society and
changes steadily. There is by no means one standard
pronunciation of the long "i" (e.g. my mind)
among the best speakers of the present day.

Much of what has been said applies to local or
common grammatical errors. Good English in
this sense should be expected in public speech.
The common errors are not really numerous,
though they are very difficult to eradicate : plural
nouns with singular verbs, the use of " seen,"
" done," etc., for " saw," " did," etc., are perhaps
the most widespread. Pronouns are used in an odd
way in the West. It is remarkable that in the
North, where " thou " and " thee " remain in the
dialect, children already feel so far on their best
behaviour in school that they will not use these
pronouns before the teacher. A besetting sin of
some teachers is to be too pedantic in insisting on
grammatical accuracy, where good vernacular
conversational English no longer does so. " He is
the man whom I met " is technically correct but it
is not nowadays good vernacular English. The
teacher's own speech, in this respect as in that of

pronunciation, should be a pattern as far as he can make it so. But this does not mean a stilted English, artificial and unreal. He can be racy on occasion, but need not be slangy. He can also speak literary English on occasion without being pompous and affected

Reading.

Particulars of the various methods of teaching reading now in vogue may be found in the manuals specially written for teachers of young children. They cannot be described in detail here, though some observations upon them are pertinent. Apart from special methods associated with particular reading books, sometimes with special types of printing, the main methods are known as the Alphabetic, the Phonic (or Phonetic) and the Look and Say. The first is the old-fashioned mode upon which most persons now over fifty were brought up ; letters were called by their names and words were spelled by naming the letters, e.g. " see," " ay," " tee," cat. The second method calls letters by their sounds and, as different sounds correspond to the same letter in different circumstances, the learner not infrequently gets into difficulties. The third method, in reaction against the excessive attention given in the other two to the single letter, emphasises the whole word : the learner is to see and recognise " cat "—" dog " as wholes.

None of these methods is wholly satisfactory if adhered to with unrelaxing strictness. The Alphabetic Method, now much decried and practically abandoned, cannot have been without merit, if it sufficed for so many generations of persons not wholly illiterate. Its great defect was that it was slow to get under way and left many stragglers in the classes. True, the large number of children who will learn to read, and to read properly, on almost any method, made rapid progress. Although the naming of the letters had no sort of logical connection with the pronunciation of the words, the ordinarily intelligent child soon associated the sound of the word with the printed symbol, and even with the names of the letters. " C," " a," " t," did come rapidly to mean, not a word like " seeaytee," but " cat." But there were many children who perhaps remembered the words they had laboriously spelled and learnt, but who were quite unable to apply their knowledge to new words.

The Phonic Method, now almost universally adopted in some form or other, has the undoubted advantage that the children, if properly taught, are from the first not afraid to attack new words. They blunder, of course, but they learn from their blunders. The fact that the same symbol is used for various sounds is a stumbling-block. It would be less formidable if teachers recognised more clearly that the unit in English reading is the syllable, and not the letter. Irregular in its spelling as English is, there is a much greater uniformity in the syllables than is commonly supposed. Whatever the method adopted, Alphabetic, Phonic or Look and Say, the teacher should get on to the syllable as early as possible, and stress the syllable : e.g. *ake* in words like make, take or rake, and this as distinct from *ike* (like) or *oke* (poke). This advice is equally valid for the Look and Say method ; children can take in a syllable with the eye and recognise it when a long word leads to guess-work. It was because under the old-fashioned method, pupils rapidly learnt to connect their spelling with syllables, and broke words up into syllables that the logical inadequacy of spelling by letter was not felt.

Probably the best method will bring in the good points of all three, even of the Alphabetic. A Phonic method is often made too systematic, for it unfortunately happens that the most fascinating words are not reached until comparatively late. Dog and cat come in early in the Phonic scheme, but horse and cow late, and " once upon a time " later still. Hence many of the primers have to be very artificial in order to illustrate the easier sounds in the first lessons. If the primer is unreal in its reading matter, the teacher has the remedy in her own hands. As soon as the class has made a start, she should compose suitable matter for reading from the blackboard and introduce such words as are required to make good sense, saying plainly what they are, and letting the children learn them by " looking " and " saying " or even by spelling alphabetically. Blackboard work is the necessary complement to the individual method previously described. It is required also in order to repeat in fresh forms what the slender primers provide, and to give variety to the necessary drill. In fact the teacher of young children must invent or compose her own reading book. The plan here suggested, of using the blackboard freely as a supplement to primer or reading slips, is not inconsistent with the individual method ; it summarises, corrects, and confirms and fills out what the pupils have learnt at their desks.

In due time children arrive at reading from books. The early preparatory stage is over, and all the preliminary difficulties have been met. The children need practice and plenty of it. Some teachers break up the larger classes into smaller groups, each under a leader. Useful as this plan may be in moderation, it is open to the objection which was fatal to the monitorial system a century ago, that it cultivates little beyond the ready recognition of words. The reading lesson of the whole class, or of a whole section of it, under the guidance of the teacher is still an essential piece of methodical procedure.

The reading lesson requires, but does not always receive, a great deal of serious thought on the part of the teacher. Hardly any lesson has been more spoiled by convention and routine. The ultimate purpose of teaching to read is that the pupils may be able to make out, to understand, to appreciate or to act on the written or printed word. Reading is more than reading aloud, and it is more than merely going over the pages of a book silently.

As a means or instrument in acquiring the whole art of reading, reading aloud has a decided but

limited importance. It is true that a person cannot
be said to understand the sense of a piece of English,
if he cannot attempt to pronounce it aloud. But
this does not justify the predominance which reading
aloud once had in schools ; it was too often
"barking at print." Yet reading aloud has its
own value ; not, as some suppose, because the pupil
will need the accomplishment in later life to any
serious extent. Reading aloud to an audience, large
or domestic, is not an art for everyone, and, to be
well done, needs a kind of training which it is neither
necessary nor possible to give to all pupils. The
value of reading aloud may perhaps be described
by saying that the practice is an indispensable
instrument in learning the native tongue, a means
by which pupils may discover their own shortcomings (for they do not know some words), while
the teacher may gauge the progress of his class and
find out what he has still to teach. The lesson in
reading aloud gives the teacher opportunities of
enlarging the English vocabulary of his class, of
teaching new words and phrases, of explaining them
when they are partially understood, of practising
the pupils in the ready recognition of familiar words
and phrases, of correcting mispronunciations and
bad speech ; and further, through his own reading,
of conveying, without formally trying to teach, some
impression of the rhythm, the sonority, the clearness
and the force of good English.

In conducting such a reading lesson, some cautions
should be observed. The matter to be read must
be something that is worth reading aloud. This

H

worthy matter naturally includes what good authors have written, though at times an involved passage even in a good author may be beyond the powers of the pupils. It also includes on occasions such specimens of direct English as a mathematical rule or principle clearly expressed. It does not include the matter of fact statements of a geography text book, or the curt phrases of a historical summary. At least these are not the proper material for an ordinary lesson ; not that they are not good English, but that time can be better spent on better material for the purpose. The lesson in reading aloud must be conducted with a definite conception of its object, which is, ultimately, the development of the pupil's knowledge of English. There must be no confusion with the requirements of other subjects. History, geography and science cannot be learnt by reading aloud.

Coming down to details we may recommend as follows. For the most part the children should first read over to themselves what they are to read aloud. Unseen reading is a severer test than need be imposed, especially upon beginners. They misunderstand, and pardonably misunderstand, stumble and read wrongly ; time is wasted in putting them right. This rule is not absolute ; easy dialogue for example may sometimes be attacked at sight. But it is a safe rule to follow in general. The teacher will have himself to decide when the class is to follow with book open and when with book shut, but in either case the reader must be easily and plainly audible to the whole class. The readers should mainly be those who need this practice, though good readers should be given a chance, if only as relief and pattern. The whole class should be covered regularly, but an equal amount of time should not necessarily be given to each member.

Explanations, where necessary, should be brief and direct, and the teacher should know when to tell outright the meaning of a strange word or phrase, and when briskly to get it from some forward pupil. He should beware of trying to " elicit " what is not there, and should waste no time in roundabout ways of reaching his end. He should have at his command vivid illustrative sentences in which the meaning of a word or phrase is often better conveyed than by a dictionary equivalent. Phrases are often more important than words, and ignorance of idiomatic phrases confuses a child more than ignorance of words. It is a good plan for the teacher to annotate his own copy of the reading book and prepare his explanations and illustrations in advance. As a piece of technique, it is unwise to interrupt a reader or to correct mistakes in the middle of a passage. A brief signal, given by word or hand, at a suitable point, will indicate when he is to stop. Almost any passage read will suggest to the alert teacher interesting by-ways in language and sense, which it is tempting to explore. If there is no hurry, and the time can be afforded, it is better to leave a period at the end of the lesson or to make a short interval, instead of constantly interfering with the steady flow of the lesson.

It is now generally felt that along with reading as a linguistic exercise should go the appreciation of good English literature. The young teacher engaged with classes of the primary stage will be wise not to try formal lessons on " appreciation." Direct instruction on this is all but impossible, for the kind of exposition on the literary points of a piece of good English which a skilled teacher can give to an older class is out of place with young children. They learn " appreciation " insensibly, especially if the teacher himself reads with zest, and reads well, and if they are given nothing but what is good. A properly conducted reading or recitation lesson on a poem, where the meaning is delicately brought out and the class is led to imagine what the poet imagined is in itself a lesson in appreciation. In an ordinary lesson the teacher may call on the class to admire a particularly vivid, or terse, or full, or humorous piece of English, but he should leave it at that. The pupils will best show their appreciation not by writing immature "critiques" but by reading with effect and enjoyment.

At this point a word on *recitation* is in place. The main object in view in this exercise is of course to store the memory of the children with verse of a high quality ; accordingly pieces should be carefully selected which are suitable to the age and taste of the class. They are best memorised, it is now agreed, by allowing the children to read one, or a few stanzas, again and again, and not by learning them phrase by phrase. The children should understand the poem, but this does not mean that every word and allusion need be analysed and dissected. If they are allowed sometimes to choose the poems to commit to memory, they will choose poems they do not fully understand, but enjoy all the same. They should be encouraged in this. Rhythm and the swing of verse appeal to children, and should not be forgotten in the teacher's choice. So at the right age, ballads may be suggested. But in the end the teacher must be guided by experience and not by prescription. The importance of recitation in the training of good speech has already been hinted at, and requires here no further amplification.

Reading does not end with reading aloud : rather does it begin there. The use of reading to the grown up person is for enjoyment and for information, or for both purposes combined. Clearly these ends must be kept in mind even in the primary stage, when the art of reading is being taught. There is no special technique to be recommended. If in the first years the children have been taught to expect the reading books to mean something for them, they will use books both to enjoy them and to learn from them, without suspecting they are doing anything out of the way. The fortunate ones, who come from homes with books, read story books of their own, and many of them have access to books and papers on animals or engines or other matters which interest them. The rest have to be introduced to these delights at school.

Children do not need to be tempted into reading stories for pleasure : give them the books and they will read. Reading for information, particularly reading in order to find the complete answer to some special question is not so easily achieved. In the primary stage it can be begun if the teacher refers to the book as a matter of course. " What does it say in your book ? " ought to be a usual and familiar question. So also, in a small way, even young children can be trained to gather up the sense of what they are reading in order to reproduce it orally or in writing. Experience shows that if the teacher definitely sets out to teach the art, classes readily acquire the knack of picking out the main points of a narrative, and even of a descriptive piece of writing. This is the principle advocated by the Parents' National Educational Union, whose books may be consulted by those who are specially interested.

One ought not to be writing on this matter in an apologetic tone, as if something extremely difficult and unusual were being advocated. In secondary schools it has generally been assumed that pupils could use books, and they had regularly to get up a lesson from books in order to have it heard the next day. This valuable habit has not been trained in elementary schools for the most part for the all-sufficient reasons that children took no lesson books home, and had only a limited number in school. Classes were too large for work prepared individually to be heard and tested, and with large classes the teacher was so much engaged with the mechanics of oral reading as to have little or no time for leaving the class to study for themselves. With classes now smaller, and with a more liberal supply of books, "study" becomes more feasible. If home work is not set, "preparation" can be given inside the school time-table.

The importance of teaching children to read for the purpose of getting information, of studying for themselves, cannot be over-emphasised. It is becoming felt with greater force than ever that children at the end of the primary stage should know how to read for themselves, and the methods of teaching beyond the age of eleven are founded upon the assumption that pupils can be depended upon really to "read." If a young teacher finds his class has no power to do this, he might begin by borrowing books from a class lower than his own, and setting the class to read them "for information." It is too much to expect that a child will appropriate the contents of a passage while he is wrestling with its meaning. The intimate connection between reading for study and reproduction in composition is obvious.

Composition.

Composition is not a very happy term for those exercises in speaking and writing where the pupil is repeating or inventing a story, reproducing by statement or narrative something he has learnt or read, or recording something he has observed. It suggests the formal essay or set piece, and the set piece is unsuitable for the primary stage we are considering. In this stage composition should be not a subject but a bit of ordinary natural procedure or method—one of the various means by which the pupils give back what they have learnt. It should have the same relation to lessons in geography, history and science or other oral lessons as working a set of sums has to regular lessons in arithmetic.

Teachers have sometimes made a sharp distinction between oral and written composition, and have assigned separate periods in the time-table to each. Oral composition occurs, of course, whenever a child answers or asks a question in class. It is unnecessary to devote a lesson period to the subject, provided that the teacher remembers through all his teaching to encourage readiness, clearness and some fluency in his class. He will often put questions which demand a reply in consecutive sentences, and not in one word or phrase. The best occasions for continuous oral composition are in the telling and re-telling of stories and other narratives. It is indeed on this side of the teaching in the early stage that speech in its widest senses can and should be cultivated. The teacher of the younger children will make the greatest use of stories, not only in order to enlarge the acquaintance of the children with the worlds of reality and imagination, but also to increase their power to understand and to use their own tongue. They will learn English from well-told stories better at first than from the books they read; and in telling them again, whether, as children love to do, in the actual words of the teacher, or in a version of their own, they have a genuine exercise in composition.

Accordingly not only are the right stories to be chosen, but they must be told directly and clearly, with vividness yet with economy of words, in language exactly adapted to the class (which means a little beyond the language the child will itself use at first), in a lively manner but without any exaggerated gestures or artificial tones. They must be told so that the children can re-tell them and insensibly reproduce the language of the story, or act them when they lend themselves to acting. The beginner will do well to write out her stories in full, correct them after trying to tell them, prune them of what is needless, and clear up what proves to be obscure. She should make her own collection of all kinds of stories, standard tales like the Three Bears, fairy stories like Cinderella, fables, animal stories, stories about heroes and heroines who appeal to children, stories of real life. It is to be remembered that stories, well read or well told, along with the poetry that the children will hear and learn form the beginnings of an appreciation of literature. They should not be suddenly dropped out when composition begins to be written, and the valuable training which the oral re-telling of a tale affords ought to be continued as an occasional exercise right through the primary stage.

Written composition offers certain difficulties of its own, and as it is very generally treated in schools as a special subsection of English, these must be considered. If a class has been well taught in the earlier years, it will already be accustomed to expressing its ideas in writing with a genuine individual note, albeit somewhat simply and perhaps crudely. But in many schools the difficulty will be to get the children to write at all. With pen and paper and subject all ready, they do not " know what to put down." There is nothing for it but to show them how; to ask simple questions and suggest how the answers should run, to start them on a simple story, or to tell them the first sentence or two of the description of something they are certain to know. In order to overcome the awkwardness of beginning little compositions, any kind of help is legitimate. Words may be suggested and spelt for the pupils. Faulty grammar and punctuation may be straightforwardly rectified without blame or explanation : " say this ; put it this way ; stop here and begin afresh." The main thing is to get the children going. Help of the kind mentioned is not out of place even when the class has been used to writing. For a lesson in composition must not be confused with a lesson in spelling or grammar.

Criticism by the teacher of what is written is often wholly misplaced. When it is directed at mis-spellings, at grammatical errors, at cumbrous and long sentences, at handwriting, and at these alone, it damps the willingness of the class without really improving their powers. It should be directed almost entirely at inexactness and inaccuracy in the statement of what the writer knows.

The first essential of good composition is clearness, with exactness. If the class is writing the story of St. George and the Dragon, the compositions in which the tale runs consecutively and can be followed by someone who did not know it beforehand should be praised ; others, however nicely written or correctly spelt, should be condemned if they do not tell a straight tale. The writer should be shown where his writing does not make sense ; he will be more impressed by his failure to say what he knows than by any number of pencil marks noting slips in grammar. Moreover, mistakes in grammar and mis-spellings often lead to a failure of sense, and they should be reprobated as such.

It is worth while to set special tasks, within the powers of the class, to cultivate the sense of accurate statement. Such are plain descriptions of simple objects, e.g. a button, a blackboard, an inkwell ; questions to be answered, such as : " how would you direct a stranger from school to railway station ? " or " Describe a cricket pitch when it is prepared for a game." In general, if the composition is to make sense and to be genuine, it must be upon something the class knows well and fully, and upon which it has its knowledge at command. Topics once in vogue like "Newspapers," " Town and Country life " are too vague unless they come naturally after a specific lesson on the theme. The old adage of the Roman educationist, Quintilian, cannot be mended : " Seize firmly the matter, words will follow." It is true not only as meaning that a writer will write without effort if he knows his subject, but also that he will write accurately. Many teachers give " imaginative " compositions, which seem to contradict what has been said. These have their place, and children usually enjoy them. They should not be overdone, however : the type of " Autobiography of a Cab-Horse," useful as an occasional exercise, is apt to be carried too far. When children are acquiring in various lessons an enormous amount of new and interesting knowledge, it seems a pity not to let them use it in writing, and thereby fix it more firmly in their minds.

To sum up, lessons in composition should be directed towards accuracy and clearness of statement. We must be prepared, especially in the early stages, to find some falling off in spelling and penmanship. This need not cause undue concern, since the facility will be recovered as the power of expression grows.

Spelling.

Spelling is the bugbear of the teacher in English schools. Doleful statistics are presented to show how much time is wasted in the effort to learn how to spell our irregular language correctly. Some persons point to the golden days when children really learnt to spell, it is said ; others think spelling is of no account, and others advocate systems of phonetic or otherwise simplified spelling. There is little doubt that the young teacher, whatever his private views of the matter may be, will be expected to teach his class how to spell. How shall he do it ? Spelling, for the most of us, is a mechanical art, depending on memory and association. It had better be attacked as such, and systematically taught and practised. It should be treated apart from reading and composition, at any rate in the sense that the class in these lessons must not be preoccupied with spelling.

The first obvious aim is the accurate spelling of the words the children use when they write ; this however, need not mean that the knowledge of spelling should be limited to the meagre vocabulary of a rather inarticulate pupil. The further aim, not to be accomplished by specific and direct teaching, is to train children to acquire the spelling of a word when they learn the word. If they have been well taught at the beginning, they will have written the new sets of words as they learnt them, and thus have translated the symbol into the sound, and the sound back again to the symbol. A teacher of children of seven, eight or nine would do well to review the reading primers and books and use them for spelling. It will be found that, odd as English is, there is a great deal more of regularity and rule than he would suspect. The English language does not consist wholly of words ending in "—ough." There are rules already learnt consciously or unconsciously in reading, which can be applied to spelling : for example, plan, plane, planning, planing, planned, planed. The teacher need not disdain the old jingles, such as " i before e, except after c," or other mnemonics.

As in reading, the syllable is the important element. Irregularities and exceptions there are in plenty, and to learn these, for the pupils who are not good spellers by a gift of nature, practice and written practice will be necessary. Formal lessons on the differences between *his* and *is*, *their* and *there*, *here* and *hear*, are tedious and of little real value.

Practice in writing usually means dictation, an exercise condemned much too readily because it was so much abused in the past. Dictation is a very good teaching device, as teachers of foreign languages have found out. In order to be valuable, it certainly should not be only the stereotyped dictation of a paragraph, prepared or unprepared. That is a test which is in place at an examination, but inappropriate on most other occasions. The teacher should usually compose his own dictation for the particular purpose which he has in view ; it may be a single word, or sets of words, alike or unlike, or again a phrase or a sentence ; he may sometimes read a sentence or two and expect only chosen words to be written down. Dictation as a method should be flexible and varied. It will rarely occupy a whole lesson period for it will be used to clinch a bit of teaching and fix the new words in memory.

Spelling is for most persons determined by the eye and, broadly speaking, the more they read with attention, the better they spell. But a fair number of children seem incapable of associating the sound of a word with its spelling, and for them spelling by letters and syllables seems inevitable. The teacher is likely to be troubled by mistakes in common words, like " his " or " is," " their " and " there," already mentioned. If a class regularly confuses these, the teacher should give a daily dictation for two or three minutes of sentences like " There he is," " They used their eyes," with variations, until the class is even wearied into the accurate memorising of these essentials, and until a wrong spelling " looks wrong." In all its work with spelling, the class should learn to regard mis-hearing as a more heinous offence than mis-spelling : this especially in words with " h." So a great and even an exaggerated distinctness of speech must be cultivated by the teacher in these exercises.

Grammar.

The difficulty in teaching grammar lies not so much in the method as determining what position grammar is to occupy at the primary stage. Are we to give what is called a thorough grounding in English grammar for its own sake, and in order mainly that the grammar of Latin or French may be grasped more readily later on ? Or can all that is necessary be taught incidentally in the course of reading, literature or composition lessons ?

The young teacher will have his task prescribed for him, and must devise means accordingly. He should remember one or two important principles. The English language is so flexible that it cannot be constricted within very narrow rules. No attempt, therefore, should be made, at this stage, to give precise and scientifically accurate definitions, since such definitions will be beyond the intelligence of the children. No definitions of the apparently

simple conception of a verb or of a sentence have
been devised which are at once accurate and
comprehensible to beginners ; grammarians themselves quarrel over these fundamentals.

On the other hand, no one has a good knowledge
of his native tongue who does not attach a meaning
clear enough for practical purposes, to the common
terms of grammar, such as noun, verb, sentence,
singular, masculine, comparative, passive, subject,
and predicate.   The safest course seems to be to
let the pupils learn by multitudes of examples what
these constituents and these phenomena of our
language are in practice.   A rough description,
which does not pretend to be a definition, will have
to be used.   For the purpose of giving the class the
ability to identify the parts of speech, to see at once
number, gender, tense, voice, etc., and to analyse
a sentence into subject and predicate, straightforward examples should be used.   Difficult or
ambiguous examples should be ruled out, and quite
openly set aside as too hard.

The straightforward examples may come at
first from the teacher or from the reading book.
But for the most part they should be drawn from
the children.   Once their attention has been turned
towards an examination of their own tongue, heard
and spoken every day, they can be led to take a
keen interest in it, and will be found to be extremely
fertile in supplying instances, when they have
realised what a reservoir of knowledge they have
at command.   When dealing, for example, with
the verb, they can be asked to name actions they

themselves have carried out in the process of dressing or using a cricket bat, or making a drawing : " I tumbled out of bed, I put on slippers, I took off night clothes, I fastened or buttoned my waist-coat, I chose a collar, I tied my tie, I laced my boots, etc., etc." The verb in each case is perfectly clear, and the class must be told which word is the verb proper. They may be led to describe other actions, or in a vivid narrative to pick out the lively verbs, and if they omit some which are not clear, no matter.

So they may be led to suggest adjectives which apply to some striking object, a ship, a train, a pillar box and so forth. In the same way they may be led, first to invent as many ways as possible of describing an action in the past, present and future, and then classify them into tenses : or again to discover from their own stores verbs with the past tense in " d " or " ed," and the so-called strong verbs. There is the fun of a lively game in building up the various pronouns in declensions, and the verb in a kind of conjugation. These particular technical terms are unnecessary, but the common technical terms may as well be taught as avoided. The focus of their meaning will be quite clear, and the rather wide region of the doubtful may be left aside until grammarians agree. The important thing is to bring to light and to arrange in outline the knowledge that the class already implicitly possesses.

Above all, in grammar even more than in other subjects, the teacher should beware of pedantry,

I

remembering that many phrases, which a strict grammarian would condemn, are undoubtedly part of good conversational English. No one really says " Whither are you going ? " or " It is they," and very few ask " Whom are you looking for ? " So sentences, the meaning of which is perfectly clear when they are spoken, should not be pilloried as inexact : " I want my bicycle mending, badly " is unmistakable as uttered by a speaker and need not be criticised in speech.

Analysis is commonly recommended as the right beginning of grammar. But, beyond the plain distinction between subject and predicate in straightforward sentences, it is probably too subtle for children of the primary age. Much of the old-fashioned parsing was very unreal, as well as very dreary. But a brisk labelling of the component parts of a good sentence, without the technicalities which are in place only in a highly inflected language like Latin, is a useful exercise, a legitimate sequel to the exercises advocated above. One more caution ; in his absorption with the function of single words the teacher should not forget the phrase.

CHAPTER X

ARITHMETIC AND MATHEMATICS

In discussing the teaching of reading we suggested that there should be borne in mind a distinction between the introductory stage proper and the later stage of systematic application. So with arithmetic, a useful distinction can be made between the stage in which the child is acquiring a familiarity with the elements of number, and the later stage of applying his knowledge to systematic arithmetic. The beginning must be slow if it is to be sure, and the teacher's first objective is a thorough knowledge of number up to 10.

To this end, formal class lessons alone, even if enlivened by the ball-frame and other apparatus, are of comparatively little effect. The child must gain his conception of what numbers mean, not so much by being told about them as through feeling, handling and counting things, and he must himself experiment with the things he is counting. Thus the individual methods which are so useful in the early lessons in reading are of as great value in early lessons in number. For particulars of the various ways in which individual methods are carried

acquainted with very simple problems of money and with simple measurements. Here too they should in the first instance see and handle real measures, and real or imitation coins. There is no space here to describe methods in more detail or to discuss the best modes of teaching subtraction, multiplication and division or of introducing the idea of fractions. The manuals already referred to will furnish abundant particulars. It may be remarked that in the initial stages very large numbers are not required. The essentials of the various arithmetical processes can be learnt with numbers within the range already suggested.

At this point a note on the question of tables is in place. Addition tables are no longer learnt by rote as they once were, nor is there any necessity for them. But multiplication has always been a source of vexation and according to the well-known rhyme division is as bad. It was the old practice to commit tables to memory without explanation. They were repeated without mistake and a good class would respond at once to a rapid series of questions which jumped from one table to another. Unfortunately, except with a few intelligent children, the plan gave no power to construct a new table, or to rebuild one that had been partially forgotten.

The reaction against this method has gone to an opposite extreme ; many teachers make their pupils build up tables on an intelligent plan but fail to secure their being committed firmly to memory. Thus children, otherwise capable enough, fail later on through uncertainty in such knowledge, and are accused of slowness when they merely lack the necessary groundwork for exact computation. By all means children should construct their tables, and go on beyond 12 times 12 up to 20 times 20. But they should have them firmly in memory, at any rate up to 12 times 12. It is not fair to handicap them by uncertainty on this point, and no fear of the charge of mechanical teaching or of rigid drill should deter a young teacher from insisting upon a knowledge of the tables. There is even a play element in them. It is useful also to work out tables for 20, 16, 15, 14, 25, 60 times, which will be required later on. If an upward limit is desired, products beyond 100, 144 or 200 can be excluded. Children will also strengthen their arithmetical limbs, so to say, if they practise division tables, and even tables like 3 times 1 ; 3 times $1\frac{1}{2}$; 3 times 2 ; 3 times $2\frac{1}{2}$, etc.

In due course the pupils reach classes for which an arithmetical text-book is prescribed. The young teacher must not be misled by the completeness and the orderliness of such text-books and suppose that he has little to do but follow the book. He has to remember that the business of the primary stage in arithmetic is not simple ; it is to apply the knowledge of the principles of arithmetic, acquired in an elementary form in the earlier years, to larger numbers, to sums of money, to weights and measures, to fractions, vulgar and decimal, and with this to teach more advanced ways of handling numbers and the use of computation in practical life. At the same time the importance of accuracy must be understood. Vague and imperfect conceptions of meaning in English and history, and to some extent in geography, may be pardoned in the young and immature, but there must be no indefiniteness in early arithmetic. The use of approximations comes much later.

Before offering positive suggestions on detail a general question or two must be discussed. What should be the balance between " mental " and written arithmetic ? How much should the teacher show or demonstrate and how much make the class work examples ? How far should he attempt to teach the theory of arithmetic and how far depend on rule of thumb ? How much of what they do are the children to visualise ?

Some exceptional teachers now advocate the complete abolition of arithmetic worked on paper, and say that the pupils should carry on all arithmetical operations in the head, possibly recording merely the answers. They would not begin to set down sums at an earlier age than eleven. This mode of procedure is beyond the young teacher, and is probably inconsistent with what his class will be actually required to do. It is mentioned here in order to stress the importance of mental arithmetic.

A safe rule is that as much of the working of a sum as possible should be done mentally, save when a teacher may ask for very full working so as to reveal failures in method or in accuracy. Far too much margin work is often allowed, e.g. division or multiplication which (with the answers) should be easily carried in the head, easy divisions by 20 or multiplications of small numbers by single digits. No one aims to make lightning calculators juggling with large numbers, but the capacity of average children to reckon in the head is often underrated.

" Mental arithmetic " has another meaning not to be overlooked—the rapid dealing with small problems, in money especially, the use of short methods, quick calculation generally. This useful form of gymnastic should be adequately cultivated, especially in the kind of problems that occur in the practical business of shopping and travel, but it need not become a fetish.

There is no more fascinating lesson than a good demonstration lesson in arithmetic, when the class is led on step by step to the perception of a new rule, the pupils being called upon at all points to do the actual reasoning and working and the teacher guiding by penetrating questions, and helping only when the class is at a complete loss. But the young teacher should beware of pitfalls. One brilliant lesson on the multiplication of decimals does not finally teach the class how to do these teasing sums. The class often reaches a triumphant conclusion and forgets the road to it. Immediate practice and plenty of it, frequently accompanied by partial or complete repetition, will be necessary.

Moreover, a demonstration lesson gains immensely in force, if the class is ready for it, by having reached a point at which a new rule is required. Suppose, for example, a class has had plenty of practice, especially mental practice, in adding and subtracting fractions with the same denominator, not only the easier $\frac{3}{8}+\frac{5}{8}$ type but $89/100-17/100$; $47/60+67/60$; $25/7-6/7$; and can so far handle fractions as familiarly as integers, they will appreciate (and it is to be hoped, demand) the method by which fractions with unlike denominators are added. Not all important new rules can be approached in this way, simple interest for example ; but the ground can be broken here easily enough by a reference to Savings Banks. The main thing is not to overdo demonstration on the one hand, and on the other not to let the class blunder along unintelligently for want of a little showing.

In an earlier chapter allusion has been made to " concrete arithmetic," and the misuse of the term has been hinted at. The pleas that are heard for more " concrete " and more " visual " arithmetic, arise from a perception that much of the arithmetic of the text books is unreal to children ; they have no mental image corresponding to numbers and quantities like 250, $15/16$, ·0125, 3 tons, £173, 80 miles, except the figures or words to represent them. If they have not these images, are they not merely juggling with figures ?

The young teacher need not be anxious on this account, if he will observe one or two precautions. Arithmetic, after all, is an abstract science in the main, and a constant reference to the " concrete " gets in the way of smooth and rapid working. It is a piece of common sense in the early stages to make the operations as real and concrete as possible, and later on to bring in as many practical applications as possible. Thus, in beginning money sums, they should handle coins, real or imitation, with sufficient familiarity to convince them that a half crown is a coin in actual use, that it does amount to two shillings and sixpence and that eight go to the pound sterling. So in weights and measures, especially the latter, they should, up to the limits of feasibility, handle ounces, and pounds, fill or see filled a quart jug with two pints and measure distances with wooden, tape or chain measures. They will but vaguely remember the feel of an eight ounce weight, but they can judge the capacity of a breakfast cup, and they can measure lengths and areas to an almost indefinite extent.

But the value of all these preliminary exercises is that they are for reference in the background, and not to be present in the mind when calculating the weight of a train or the speed of an aeroplane flight. So with " practical " problems, their value is to let the arithmeticians feel that they are worth while : it is somebody's business or at any rate it interests somebody to find the answers. Whether the children can guess the lapse of a minute or not is amusing but not very important ; but it is important that they should know their way very thoroughly about a clock face. A class has been known to be engaged on time sums, when not a single member of it could tell the time by a watch. The limits within which " concrete " methods can be used in a classroom are very narrow, but they should not be neglected, especially in measures of

length and area ; the playground offers chances
for experiment and calculation, and the children's
walks to and from school can, of course, be utilised.
But there is no need to invent highly artificial
problems in the effort to create an illusion of
reality.

Some suggestions may be offered on a few points
of detail. In the first place it is very important
that the pupil should thoroughly understand the
place value of the digits in our notation. This is
not to say that when he is multiplying 176×35,
he should think all the time of the value of the tens
and hundreds figures, still less that he should say
"thirty times 70 is 2,100." But he should have
at the back of his mind and at command the con-
sciousness that the 7 represents 70, the 3, 30 and the
product as he puts it down is 21 hundreds. Only
in the introductory lessons need the teacher remind
his class that the 3 they carry in an addition, the 1
they borrow or add in subtraction, represent
not always units but tens or hundreds and so on,
according to their place in the series. Once this
simple but necessary bit of theory is grasped, the
class should work away as mechanically as they
will.

Decimals will not be understood unless the place
value of integers is quite clear. From time to time
by way of revision and in order to cultivate a
readiness to handle large written numbers, the
class may read a number like 35,679 as 35 thousands,
etc., or 356 hundreds, etc., or 3,567 tens, etc. To
emphasise this arithmetical intelligence—and to

avoid careless blunders—many teachers begin a multiplication sum with the digit in the multiplier of highest value, and again, in a division sum they place the items of the quotient as they are reached over the last digit in the quotient which is being

$$\begin{array}{r} 3652 \text{ (and 10 over)} \\ \hline 16)58442 \end{array}$$

divided, thus :

The importance of all this in decimals need not be more than mentioned.

If, as has been justly claimed, the mathematics lesson affords an admirable training in English, it is obvious that extreme accuracy of statement is essential. To write an answer in division such as 2,163 shillings $\frac{1}{4}$ 20 in the form £108+3 instead of £108 and 3 shillings over must be forbidden. So also equations generally must really equate : $37+48-26+18-11=37+48+18=103-26-11=66$ is not permissible at all, even if the answer is right. So statements in " problems " must be exact, though they can be abbreviated, as they should be.

Something has already been said about the handling of concrete material. Young teachers are lightheartedly told to let their classes learn their fractions " practically." The advice is sound enough, but not at all easy to carry out. The obvious way is by making the children measure lines and areas and fractions of these. But a common mistake is to have the units too small, the inch for example. The common foot rule with its inches, half, quarter and eighths of an inch, or its tenths or twelfths,

invaluable as it is in its place, is perhaps responsible
for some confusion when used to demonstrate the
meaning of fractions. The fractional parts are
almost too small to be seen. It is better to take a
plane figure, a square or perhaps even more useful
an oblong, and let the children experiment with
that. They are not yet to find their way to the
rule for adding fractions of unlike denominators, but
to grow familiar with fractions, and no longer to shy
at the customary method of writing them. Fractions
like $\frac{7}{8}$, $\frac{5}{6}$, $\frac{11}{12}$, $\frac{9}{16}$, $\frac{17}{20}$, should be as readily named and
dealt with as integers. It is better to keep the
nomenclature five-sixths and not to confuse beginners
with the notion of one-sixth of five. This, and the
still more difficult conception of five sixths as
expressing ratio should be left till the next stage.
When the first strangeness of fractions has been
overcome, the children will be ready to begin
exercises in fractions which involve the four rules.

A concrete way of approaching decimals is to
let the class construct on paper a few largish squares,
dividing them longitudinally into tenths, and later
by horizontal division into tenths to make hundredths.
It is then easily possible by shading parts of the
square to show the class what $\cdot3$, $\cdot14$, etc., look
like, and what they mean ; and so with $\cdot03$, $\cdot07$,
$\cdot26$, $\cdot61$ and the like ; the bright boy of the class
will himself invent a simple method of indicating
on his square $\cdot125$ or $\cdot635$. But for the main part,
the teaching of decimals will have to be abstract,
and will depend for its success on a thorough understanding of place values.

The early lessons on arithmetic should ensure as much facility as possible in the mechanical processes of addition, subtraction, multiplication and division, with a complete mastery of the necessary tables. It is waste of time to dwell on reasons at this stage, and it is not essential to wait until the perfect method of teaching every simple rule has been discovered. Skill and familiarity are more important than elaborate reasons or efforts at explaining. In making use of the skill gained by such practice the pupils will work out problems and applications of rules. Here explanation is desirable. Thus, when the time comes for working sums in interest, there should be a reason given for every step. A mere formula is not enough. On the other hand, a complete knowledge of a formula and its basis will be of little help if the pupil breaks down in such things as multiplication or division. Therefore we must seek accuracy in computation by repeated exercises, putting explanations, and theory, in their proper order as they become requisite.

CHAPTER XI

Introductory.

SINCE speech, reading, drawing, arithmetic and writing are the implements of learning, they must be used upon suitable material. History, geography, elementary science and languages may fitly be looked upon as this material, from the time when they begin to be treated as separate subjects. The foundations will have been laid in the earlier years, those of history in some of the stories of the first period, those of geography and science in the miscellaneous talks which will have accompanied the stories in conversation lessons. Side by side with tales of real and imaginary happenings, the teacher of the younger children will give lessons on things, lessons with objects and pictures, and chats upon all kinds of interesting phenomena met with at home or in the world outside.

" Object lessons " is too narrow a term for this kind of teaching, and a certain type of lesson, which attempts to exhaust the characteristics of a particular object displayed before the class in a specified period, is liable to be stereotyped and dull. What is wanted is to continue under school conditions the mode in which a child brought up in a good home acquires an immense mass of knowledge of the world around him. The knowledge is miscellaneous, and it is obtained incidentally and intermittently. It is gained by such a fortunate child by conversation, in which the child's own questioning plays a con-spicuous part ; through picture-books and toys ; through companionship with elders and through travel. Though miscellaneous, it is none the less genuine and valuable, for the child is not yet ready for systematic and orderly learning.

The best home conditions cannot be reproduced in school, but the school can imitate them in some essentials. School procedure must be more orderly, but it should not be made too formal. Thus, instead of set lessons on a flower or a plant or a bird, the children may be asked to make occasional or periodical observations, especially where growth is to be noted. The march of the seasons, with the changing aspects of weather, plants, birds and animals, lends itself especially to this kind of observation. Another kind occurs when children are told beforehand what to look for in some of the common phenomena of the town, village or street, to report what they have noticed about trains, trams or other vehicles, or about the work of the tradesman, the postman, or the policeman. The set lesson will have its place when the teacher will gather together the observations of the class and weave them into a connected description or into a narrative.

K

Even the object lesson, sparingly used, can be employed with advantage, for in it the teacher can not only permit the children to observe but also show them what they should observe, and suggest to them the questions they should ask themselves and the teacher. This is the best method of training observation, by directing the open-eyed curiosity of the children into channels which begin to be orderly and regular. Thus the ideas of contrast and comparison may be introduced and a new stimulus given to the child's own inquiries. Lessons of the kind described, while conveying information by the way, are not mere information lessons, pure and simple. Consequently they are certainly not to be revised and confirmed like the multiplication table, and children should not be examined on such lessons, as they may later be examined on their knowledge of geography. If after two or three years of such lessons on things, the children keep their curiosity undimmed and their thirst for fresh knowledge still active, and if they have not only picked up a good deal of various information but have retained a lively interest in the world that surrounds them, they will be ready and able to profit by systematic instruction in history, geography and science.

History.

There is no such agreement on the methods of teaching history in the primary stage, or even beyond, as there is concerning geography. It is sometimes even doubted whether systematic history can be taught at all to children up to eleven in the sense in which systematic geography undoubtedly can. Experts also dispute whether the early lessons should aim at giving the classes a framework of leading facts with dates, which may be filled in later on, or whether emphasis should be laid on the social life of the English people to the neglect of reigns, dates, politics and conquests ; and, again, whether an outline of world history should not precede the regular study of English history.

The young teacher will find these questions settled for him by his syllabus, and by the books he may be expected to use. He must make the best of it. If he is asked to include dates that appear to him to have no meaning for the class, let him nevertheless see that the pupils learn them with such help as he can provide in the form of time-charts and other devices. No one nowadays seriously expects the young historian to know by rote the dates of a large number of events such as the battles in the Wars of the Roses. The dates when prominent personages, Alfred, The Conqueror, Edward I, Henry V and other great monarchs, with Becket, the Black Prince, Bruce, Cranmer and others flourished or when great events occurred (1066, 1215, 1415, 1649, 1759, 1815, 1832 and 1914) are not so numerous that to learn them as they come is a task to be groaned over.

For the rest, the teacher must make the history live. After all, it is a story, and the interest of children in well told stories is perennial. In discussing other subjects we have urged that the class should be encouraged to work at exercises and to engage in investigations of their own. Though this principle is not to be forgotten, history teaching in the primary stage will be mainly a matter of oral teaching. If the teachers are talking less in other lessons, they may quite properly take the floor in the history lesson, and cultivate a vivid power of narrative. The Conquest, the struggles between King and Church, and between Parliament and King, the growth of the Empire, the Industrial Revolution, can be made of thrilling interest by an able teacher ; they may be unspeakably dreary if the teaching be spiritless.

But the teacher must not be content merely to be vivid and to let the thrill evaporate ; he must see that the class gives back the substance in some form, in speech or writing or drawing. He can also bring in the class by setting them to read in their history book the subject of his lesson, either before or after he has given it. In a modest way they can prepare for him beforehand, by finding answers to questions suggested from the book ; his own exposition will gain when he makes the dry bones of the book live. As in geography, he must avail himself of all kinds of illustrations ; the drama, ballads, contemporary accounts where these really throw light on the matter and are not simply material for the researcher ; pictures, especially reproductions of contemporary prints and manuscripts, picture postcards from the British and other museums, and extracts from historical novels.

Nor must he forget local history. The hunting out of local history, so useful at a slightly later stage, is hardly for the younger children. But even these can be given a sense of the past where opportunity offers by seeing an ancient church or castle, an old cottage or some of the relics of an older age that still remain. They can be led to see something of the course of history, in considering institutions, office holders, and occupations such as the local Mayor and Corporation, the police, the game keeper, the shepherd, the lifeboatman, their own school and its governors.

Some teachers use what is called the " Play Way " in history. The class acts the striking scenes, and the members of it compose the necessary dialogue. Done with real zest and a complete forgetfulness of the inevitable incongruities, this method is undoubtedly successful. The pupils construct their own accessories, usually in their own time, and in order to do so must engage in a simple and valuable form of research. But the method must be used with caution lest it degenerate into absurdities or be a game which is exhausted in the playing of it. The young teacher will be well advised to wait until he is sure of the class and of himself before he embarks upon it.

The teacher of history at this stage has to combine two things which are not after all incompatible : a certain precise knowledge, without which wide generalisations are useless, and a sense of history, a feeling which cannot be easily analysed, of the great movements of the human race and of our own people, of the past that is still living and of the present that is as historical as the past.

Geography.

With Geography we reach a fairly clearly defined subject, now taught on lines which are generally accepted as sound. Probably the young teacher has himself been taught on the modern method, and not in the older way now discredited.

It is usual to begin with a survey of people of other lands and, instead of bare definitions, to introduce children to geographical conceptions through pictures, modelling in clay, or by visits of observation and oral description. Following this, systematic study begins, sometimes working first from the home country, sometimes through the main geographical regions of the world. Maps have a different purpose from the one they used to serve. Once they were shown almost exclusively for topography, to teach children where on the globe the important oceans, mountains, rivers, towns, etc., were. Now children are expected in a simple way to read maps, to infer from the data they exhibit consequences and results, the productions and industries of a region, the modes of approach and transport, and the like. They are to be familiar with the method of showing height of land and depth of sea and to find for themselves the route by which a river reaches the sea.

This humanistic geography is very sound, and the young teacher should keep its aim closely in view. But he should not aim at training scientific geographers. From the maps usually available for school use, young children cannot be trusted to deduce conclusions of much value. They will not themselves and unassisted be competent to infer the productions of Wales from its mountains, or the corn of East Anglia from its climate and configuration. The skilled teacher will link the two together, physical conditions and natural productions, and connect the two in the pupil's memory ; they will perceive the connection, but should not be expected to make it at their age, for it is a scientific step much beyond their years. The real work of the teacher in the primary stage is to see that his class acquires a body of sound, full and accurate geographical knowledge, and that this knowledge is not an array of miscellaneous facts, but an orderly series in which fact is related to fact, so far as possible, by cause and effect and the facts are somehow associated with the life around the school, the homes of the children and their country. In conveying this knowledge, and in putting his pupils in the way of mastering it for themselves, the teacher will prepare them for a fuller realisation of the great ideas which constitute geography as a science.

Such a task calls for all the skill of the teacher. Suppose he is to teach the geography of Australia. He will first collect from his class what they know of the island continent from common talk and their previous reading or lessons, the importance of Australia in the Empire, its help in the Great War, the visit of the King's son to open the Parliament at Canberra, the famous cricket teams, the food which we get from Australia and so on. All this is not to tabulate information but to make it clearly worth while to study this important Dominion. Its situation in the Southern Hemisphere will suggest questions about its climate, which can be answered only by a careful examination of its configuration and a general account of the surface. The absence of great navigable rivers, the position of the few mountain ranges, the enormous elevated and dry interior and south coast, the contrasts between the semi-tropical north and the temperate south-east, all these and other salient features will be discussed and described ; and not only discussed, but noted by the class in notebooks and on blank maps of their own. The teacher must rely on his own powers of description, on passages from books of travel, on pictures and photographs to prevent his lessons from becoming a dry catalogue of gazetteer information. He will probably best present the towns, industries and population through the story of the exploration, not failing to notice the odd mixture of names, Dutch, English and native. The trade of Australia with the world and especially with ourselves will be pointedly brought home by reference to Australian mutton, fruits and wine. He will find time to go down occasional byways, to describe the interesting animal and bird life, the goldfields and mining camps, the squatters, their life and their troubles, the rough pioneer days, Botany Bay, the enterprise of crossing the Central desert, the rabbit pest, the sailing routes, and, if his class seems ready for it, even a little of the political life of the various states.

All along he will call for the active help of his class. They must not only hear about Melbourne and Sydney, the Blue Mountains and the Murray River, but know where they are, and be able to place them correctly upon a map ; they must be encouraged to hunt for information, to gather pictures and above all to be constantly asking " Why ? " and endeavouring themselves to find the answer. If the class has studied India and South Africa before, points of comparison should constantly be made, and, of course, the differences and resemblances between the new country and the old should be always in mind and mentioned often. How much reference should be made to the meteorological side of geography at this stage is not very clear. Probably not much until the pupils are old enough to watch and record barometer and thermometer readings and to appreciate the meaning of rainfall returns.

The early stage of geography teaching as treated briefly in the foregoing will be seen to call for emphasis upon things necessary to be known, such as facts in topography. These are the basis of the subject, and it is unwise to neglect them in favour of premature attempts to show reasons and causes. The facts should, however, be surrounded by an atmosphere of reality. The children should never be allowed to forget that in learning the names of geographical features they are learning the names of places where people live and work. Something of the life and work should be described, and this in a manner which may be developed later into the more scientific consideration of the influence of surroundings upon the life of mankind.

Elementary Science.

It has been felt for many years that children of the primary age should have instruction of a general kind independent of the subjects whose content is well-defined. No satisfactory name has been found for this type of instruction. " Object Lessons " will no doubt be included, but such lessons do not cover the whole of the field, nor is the kind of teaching associated with them always suitable. The term " Elementary Science " is not quite fair to the scientist, since children of this age, though they should lay foundations upon which future instruction in science can be based, are not ready for the true scientific approach. " Nature Knowledge " and " Nature Study " are hardly adequate terms, as they seem to leave out engines and machines, which, in some classes, can appropriately be introduced in an elementary way. The German word " Realien " (i.e. *real* things) has no exact English equivalent, nor does a literal translation of the French " leçons de choses " commend itself.

The aims of the course are clear. One is to satisfy the children's curiosity concerning the things around them, and to cultivate a habit of inquiring into these, and of noticing their characteristics. Another is to supply information, or better, to put the children in the way of getting it for themselves by observation and inquiry, not because they should possess the information, but because they ought to be seeking it.

Such a course will vary greatly between school and school, according to the opportunities that are offered, and according to the tastes and abilities of the teacher. Ordinarily it should include in country schools, a study of the common objects and phenomena of the countryside, and in town schools, such of these as are available. The town child cannot study wild birds or wild flowers in their natural surroundings, but can study flowers, plants and even trees in cultivated surroundings, parks, gardens, flower-pots and plant-pots. The common objects and sights of streets and highways can be studied with effect.

There remains the vast field of elementary science, the weather, the common properties of matter in its various forms, air, water, minerals, metals, materials. There is a real embarrassment of riches. In the selection, the young teacher, who may have the choice left very largely to himself, should keep in mind the desirability of having some kind of system. Not that a whole year's list should always turn on one general subject, but that lessons should be linked in groups, so that the class can feel that they have won a body of connected knowledge relating to plants, flowers, birds, metals, the sources and uses of water, and so on. To jump from the house sparrow to the gas-lamp and then to the daffodil is absurd.

The method will depend upon the particular type which is in hand. Sometimes the lesson will be a plain and straightforward talk on an object, such as a clock, or an oil lamp, brought in for the purpose. At other times it will bring together and amplify observations which the class will have been asked to make at home or on their way to school, concerning railway engines, signals or trucks. Often it will not be a formal lesson at all, but the observation continued from day to day, or from week to week, of changes of weather, the growth of trees or plants, the progress of the seasons. Sometimes again, unless the course is narrowly limited to things actually visible and tangible, it may be an " information lesson," illustrated by pictures of interesting animals and birds like the elephant, kangaroo or ostrich, or of important happenings in the world at large.

Throughout this work the class should be called on to help and contribute as much as possible, and as in other lessons, they should in some way give back what they receive. Sometimes they can be encouraged to bring their mechanical toys, if they have them, and to explain their working ; to collect appropriate illustrations and inquire about things from their parents and friends ; to make records and very simple notes, and to write simple summaries. The best form of Class Museum is probably one that is filled and emptied each year by the class itself. When the matter under treatment is flowers and plants, the class must be told they must not destroy what cannot be replaced, and, even if they can legitimately pick flowers, not to bring extravagant quantities, or to damage plants and shrubs. The windfalls in all seasons in a leafy suburb or a not too well swept park will furnish informative collecting work for a class for one year. If the school has a garden there are obvious occasions for first-rate observation and teaching.

The lessons in elementary science should be illustrated by the simplest apparatus. A cheap tin bottle, in which a little water has been heated over a spirit lamp, and, upon which, after it has been securely corked, cold water is suddenly poured, will illustrate atmospheric pressure as well as a battery of flasks and bunsen burners. The children have not yet arrived at the test-tube kind of science.

As in other subjects at this stage certain facts must be thoroughly well-known, but the time for systematising is not yet. It is best to aim at arousing interest in the surroundings of the pupils, and at offering such explanations as will lead them to further inquiry for themselves. Do not attempt to turn the observations and simple experiments into a kind of scientific ritual, or to present facts in a strictly logical order. The present purpose is that of fostering curiosity, and of satisfying it in a manner appropriate to the needs of a child.

CHAPTER XII

LANGUAGES

SOME young teachers, especially in private schools and preparatory schools, may be required to teach elementary Latin or French. In schools beyond the primary stage languages are usually, and quite properly, in the hands of specialists. It is not within the scope of this book to discuss specialist teaching, but some general suggestions may be offered for those who without specialist knowledge are called upon to teach another language than English.

Broadly distinguished, there are two methods of teaching a living foreign language, the Direct Method and the traditional method with grammar book and exercises. In the pure form of the Direct Method all the teaching is given from the beginning in the new language. Pupils learn the meaning of words and phrases not through their English equivalents, but by actions, pictures and conversation in the language. Thus the grammar of French is learnt much as a French child learns its own grammar. There is no translation into or from French.

It is clear from this rough description that none but experts, those who are not only very much at home in French but also have a firm grasp of the procedure and of the purpose of the method, can teach on the unmodified Direct Method. A teacher with a good knowledge of the rudiments can make shift and teach them on the traditional method, if he must, but the Direct Method is not for him to attempt. The price of failure is too high. On the other hand, what we have called the traditional method, modelled on long established modes of teaching Latin, is rarely followed in its crude form, nowadays, at any rate, in good schools.

The young teacher will probably find that a method which combines the features of the two is required of him. He will be expected to pronounce French with some accuracy, and to teach it perhaps through phonetics ; to use a certain amount of French in teaching, and to attempt to make his class speak French, or at least, to grow familiar with useful phrases and locutions. If the young teacher is at a loss how to introduce French speech, because he does not himself converse readily in simple French, he might well begin by using French for the ordinary class commands, instructions and questions. The fact that these occur in the same form again and again is an advantage, and the class, once familiar with the ordinary phrasing, will be ready to detect the variations that can be worked in. Where the pure Direct Method is not employed, it is better to recognise frankly that the French learnt will be learnt mainly by eye and not by ear, and to see that the pupils know and can write the phrases that are used. As a further means of accustoming the class to the sound of French, grammatical terms may as well be in French as in English—le present de l'indicatif, le pronom, etc.

A lesson in French (as in Latin) requires very careful planning in the elementary grades. It should not be confined to " construe " or to grammar or to composition, nor to conversation only—save where it is a very short lesson. It need not, however, include all these. A good type of lesson for beginners in the language, who, we will assume, have done some home work, would be : the home work exercise rapidly corrected by the class themselves (to be collected and reviewed later by the teacher), questions arising out of it or suggested by it on vocabulary or grammar, the next exercise looked at and the new points explained, some oral translation from the French portion ; perhaps a sentence for dictation or a bit of conversation on a wall-picture, or even a French song.

The grammar must be very thoroughly learnt, especially the conjugations. The class must be taught the seriousness of such blunders, as " à le," " de les." Some teachers try to impress rules on the pupils' minds. Rules are necessary, it is true, but good French is not composed by rule and only by rule. Thus the adjective should be placed after the noun, not blindly and merely because it is the rule, but because " la jaune robe " does not sound like French. It is only the constant habituation to phrases correctly expressed which will make firm the associations that must be established. Examples are la maison, je vous donne, montrez-moi, aux garçons, and a thousand other phrases which must be thought of and learned as wholes. So grammatical and other errors must look wrong when written and sound wrong when spoken.

The young teacher will be guided in the general progress of the teaching by the book that is used. He must not forget to revise constantly and if he finds that some exercises in the book are constructed to illustrate some particular point only, he should compose amalgamated exercises to combine the earlier idioms with the later. If he is to take his work seriously, and is not already a good French scholar, he must extend his own knowledge of phonetics, pronunciation and conversation, if possible under guidance.

Practice in French conversation is extremely difficult to conduct satisfactorily, even with small numbers. But an ingenious teacher, apart from the incidental conversation arising out of exercises and class orders, will find ample material in the class room itself, in pictures, and in the common actions of daily life, for extending the vocabulary of his pupils and making them use it. The ability to converse without being stilted or limited will be fostered if some common verbs in the most frequently used tenses are learnt early. Variety in phrasing should be encouraged. Thus it is not necessary to put all questions in the words " Qu'est-ce que c'est que." The miscellaneous nature of these suggestions indicates, only too clearly, that there are few cut-and-dried rules for teaching a foreign language. Here, as elsewhere, the teacher must devise his own method, taking care that he and his pupils work harmoniously together, each performing his own part.

In Latin and Greek the traditional methods hold the field at present. There is no conversation in the dead tongues, and translation from and into them has the sanction of immemorial usage. Some specially skilled teachers do indeed follow the Direct Method in these as in the living languages and bring it to a fine point. But for the most part Latin and Greek are treated as literary languages, and not as languages for day to day domestic use. The young teacher, unless he is placed in a school where the Direct Method is followed, and where doubtless he will receive instruction in the mode of using it, will be well advised to proceed on the usual method on which he has probably himself been taught.

Some of the suggestions made as to modern languages apply equally to the classical languages, the careful planning of each lesson, so that there is variety without the lesson being merely a hotch-potch, the insistence on accurate grammatical knowledge, the heinousness of some forms of error, such as are called "howlers." In Latin there is much formal grammar to be learnt at the outset in the declensions and conjugations. But the best books in use associate the grammar at once with the practical employment of it in sentences and even in simple continuous prose. So though Latin is mainly literary the best modern books are in no hurry to introduce Cæsar or Ovid, but seek to show that Latin can be employed, as of course it can, to delineate the commonest features of everyday modern life.

From the beginning the teacher should lead his class to assume that Latin really has meaning and makes sense, and show them that in its essence it is clear and unmistakable. It has too often been taught as if it were a jig-saw puzzle, the construction of which is determined by complicated rules. It would be of some help towards the real understanding of Latin even at the very beginning and certainly later on, if the class were made to read Latin in the order in which it is written, and not to hunt after the verb at the end before examining what precedes it. To a Roman " Balbus " with its clear ending in -us meant something very definite, much as the first noun in a similar English sentence does ; " murum " meant again something definite—we are doubtless going to hear something that Balbus does, did or will do to the wall, though whether he will climb, destroy, build or merely look at it, is not yet told us : " ædificat " clinches the sentence and completes it. In some German sentences we feel that a word of action is coming to complete the meaning, for which the stage is partly set by the words that come first. So the Roman anticipated the verb because he knew from the accusatives and datives, the adverbs or other phrases and clauses that a final and often a powerful determining word was to end the sentence.

This kind of anticipation can usefully be cultivated from the beginning. " Regina," clearly the agent ; " filiæ," doubtful, probably " to her daughter," because " the daughter's queen " is not good sense and a second (plural) nominative, though good sense, is odd without an " et " ; " rosam " removes the doubt, for the queen is to bring the rose in some way in touch with her daughter ; " dat," as one expected, it is a gift. The suspense in which " filiæ " is kept must have been felt as much by Roman hearers as by English, though they were hardly conscious of it.

The great amount of formal grammar to be learnt amply justifies the use of aids to the memory. Two examples may be mentioned. The old Latin primer printed the conjugations in a framework covering two opposite pages : on one were all the tenses formed from the present stems, on the other all the tenses from the perfect stems, while the subjunctives were printed side by side with the corresponding tenses of the indicative. This was of great advantage to at least one beginner. The troublesome subjunctives had always the same fixed places in the picture, and one could summon up the image of a whole verb without effort. This is something more than a mere mnemonic, for it has sound principles behind it. In a similar way declensions can be so learnt on a consistent plan that some of their difficulties are diminished. Again in learning, not only vocabulary, but also the principal parts of the regular as well as of the irregular verbs, English derivatives can be recalled, monitor to fix " monitum," caution to fix " caveo, cautum," capture for " capio, captum " and so on. Interest will be added if the connection between Latin and French is incidentally mentioned, and the connection between English and the two languages, e.g. " étang," " stagnum," " stagnant." The pupils are too young for systematic philology, but occasional scraps will enliven a lesson, and, though they may mislead every now and then, they will assist the memory.

A remark on the correction of exercises will not be out of place. The best method is for each boy to correct his own from the fair copy, put on the blackboard by teacher or scholar, or coming from the lips of the teacher. This is not suggested as the best method merely because it may save the teacher time and trouble, but because it trains the pupil to read his own exercises critically, an accomplishment not too common even among older people. If the pupil writes the correct form of the word or phrase in which he has blundered, he is more impressed than if he merely sees a mark in red or blue pencil, even with a marginal objurgation. But there are cautions to be observed in using this plan. It is more suitable for translations into the language, than for translations into English, which are better as a rule done orally. Its use is limited to exercises of a simple kind, suitable to the stage we are considering, and it can hardly be applied to prose compositions, where alternative renderings begin to be possible. General honesty in the class is, of course, presupposed. But the teacher must himself look over the corrected exercises rapidly, both to check dishonesty in individuals and, more important, to detect carelessness and to maintain a standard of accurate correction, as well as to ascertain how well or ill the exercise has been written.

In teaching languages revision must be constant and regular. The object of it is more than ascertaining that a particular construction is known or a particular book has been properly understood. It is to be sure that the class has at command the body of accurate grammatical knowledge they have once committed to memory. In proceeding to translation and composition, the pupil is no doubt always revising, but his progress is halting and uncertain if he has not the elements ready for immediate recall. Revision of the Latin declensions and French irregular verbs is wearisome, but the drudgery is well repaid by the confidence it ensures.

CHAPTER XIII

PREPARATION AND EXAMINATIONS

" In one school the class prepares the lesson and the teacher hears it ; in another the teacher prepares the lesson and the class hears it." In an earlier chapter young teachers have been advised to fall into neither of the extremes described in this saying, but to aim at the advantages that each kind of teaching carries with it. Enough has been said already as to the way in which the teacher should prepare. What of the pupil ? The answer seems easy where homework is the regular rule, since tradition, based on long and sound experience, prescribes the types of homework that can best be set, such as exercises in translation, examples in arithmetic, spellings, tables, declensions and conjugations, the " getting up " of chapters in history or geography, and occasional composition exercises. But even these commonplace activities are not to be haphazard. The amount to be set must be proportionate to the time allotted, the teacher keeping in mind that four sums well done are better than eight done hastily and probably wrongly. It is safe to work to the average boy's capacity ; the more rapid worker may fairly profit by his ability, and get through his homework sooner, if he cannot be given a special task ; the slower boys may well be told to work carefully and show up what they have been able to do in the time by a conscientious effort.

The purpose of the particular task should be before the teacher ; it may be just practice in sums and translations, or revision of work gone through already, in history or geography, or new work to be learnt in spelling or grammar, or a first run through new work in history or geography, or a piece of literature, or again a fair copy from rough notes taken in class. The rules of the school will assign the amount of time which a particular class must spend on homework, and probably the sub-jects which are to be taken on particular days. It will rest with the teacher to see that the time is well employed. Formal " preparation " is some-times a definite part of the time-table of schools where there are no tasks set to be done out of school ; the homework, so to say, is done at school in " Prep." periods, during which no class teaching takes place. But in elementary schools, and perhaps elsewhere, this kind of work has been allowed to drop to a large extent, not only as homework, but as a means of learning. It is a pity, for to set a class to master a particular piece of work and for this to be tested is salutary discipline in the best sense of the word.

Where pupils do no formal preparation at home or in school the teacher can give the task at any time and make it as long or as short as he thinks useful. The setting of definite preparation exercises, where the class really prepares for future teaching, is a flexible kind of method of which a skilful teacher can make great use. In reading, for example, where the piece cannot with advantage be taken unseen, even young classes ought to prepare. There is no reason why they should not go over in a preliminary way chapters in geography and history ; and a forward class can be set to see what they can make of a new rule in arithmetic from the directions in the book. It is obvious, as has been said, that certain things must be learnt and not only " taught," and if they cannot be learnt out of school, they must be learnt in school. In elementary schools classes are often given lessons to learn, as they are set to do exercises, but the conception of " preparation " is not as common as it should be.

Correction of Exercises.

No piece of the teacher's work is more difficult to advise upon than the correction of written exercises or sums. Some suggestions have already been made upon this subject in passing. They may now be discussed more fully. On the one hand, in a large class the personal correction of every piece of writing that is done means labour, the magnitude of which is apt to make the teacher limit the amount of written work which otherwise he would feel it right to give. And he may well doubt sometimes whether his pains are not wasted, because the careless pupils pay so little regard to his corrections and emendations. On the other hand, slackness in supervision, or an easy-going acceptance of work that may be full of errors, clearly would bring intolerable consequences. In this department of classroom work, as in others, the right advice seems to be to keep in view the purpose and object of correction in general and of each particular occasion for correction. The teacher must know what his class is doing, and whether they have really understood his teaching or taken hold of what they have learnt themselves. The class also must know where they have gone wrong, and where they have been right. To have an exercise done and not adequately dealt with when it is shown up is to incur waste of time, if nothing worse.

The following more particular suggestions may be made. The class should be trained to correct their own exercises as far as possible, that is to mark mistakes from oral correction or from fair copies on the blackboard, each pupil dealing with his own work. This practice has been recommended in the section on language teaching and discussed there. It can be applied in other subjects ; answers to written sums, to mental arithmetic where only the result is noted, dictation, tables, spelling, questions in geography and history requiring an exact answer in a few words, or to poetry written out. It cannot be applied to drawing or to arithmetic where the method is important, or to composition when this is on a general subject or is a longer answer to a question in history or geography. The teacher should rapidly scan the corrected exercises, not only to gauge the extent of the errors but to check carelessness and detect possible dishonesty. In arithmetic, the rapid correction of sums by the class will leave time for the teacher to look at the wrong answers and deal with them. Even in exercises in which the class usually marks its own, he should from time to time unexpectedly take a batch already marked and examine them critically.

Composition is particularly difficult to deal with. Full-dress corrections of the whole of the work probably ought to be more frequent than is necessary with exercises which admit of more mechanical correction. But the purpose of the exercise will often be served if half a dozen compositions are selected at random and carefully criticised before the class, their good points receiving as much attention as the bad ones. Such criticism, skilfully done, will make any minute examination of the rest unnecessary. The teacher should have a carefully devised scheme of signs to denote the kind of mistake made, error in spelling, grammar, or idiom, and also the venial mistake : but these signs should be few, for too many hieroglyphics puzzle and confuse. The teacher should know when not to mark an expression as wrong, or a sentence as poor, and, as far as he can, he should concentrate on the particular faults he wishes at the moment to eradicate.

It is not so hard to decide what should follow or accompany the corrections. Single word answers, in spelling and also in dictation, should be rewritten accurately on the spot. Answers in arithmetic should be marked wrong and left ; where desirable, the whole sum should be done again, or if a long sum, and the pupil can find where he has gone wrong, the rest of the sum. Sometimes an essay test may be done again, if a class has gone wholly astray, say, in the description of some familiar object, and the teacher has shown them how such a topic should be treated. But, unless as a pure disciplinary measure, compositions should not be rewritten ; a better plan is to call for a composition on a similar topic.

Examinations.

The foregoing suggestions lead to a consideration of examinations. Teachers are called on to examine their classes from time to time under the supervision of and for the information of the head of the school. For their own purposes also they wish to test their classes. There is an art in examining and also an art in interpreting the results. A common mistake is to confuse two kinds of tests. One is where the teacher, as part of his planned procedure in teaching, reviews a section of the work done before he feels he can go forward. The other is a periodical—usually a terminal—examination on the whole course, intended, like the first, to ascertain the success of the work of the period, but also intended to assess the individual performances of the pupils, for the purpose of promotion, report, class order, perhaps even prizes.

The differences in aim will determine differences in setting the tests. For the terminal or annual examination, where the pupils are to be strung out in order of merit, the test should be devised so that the abler members are stretched, as it were, and the less able can gain some credit upon easier questions. Arithmetic affords the best illustration : a good arithmetic paper will contain a number of straightforward sums on which all but the complete duffers will score, and also harder sums, increasing in difficulty, so that only the cleverest can attack them with success. Other subjects can be treated in a similar way, if not quite so thoroughly. A good test so constructed, with a normally good class, ought to produce results in which no one, unless the class has had to include a quite hopeless member, will earn no marks, the solid average members will gain respectable medium marks, and the few brilliant soar up to 80 or 90 per cent. The teacher should settle what he regards as a pass mark which the large majority should achieve. If they fail to do so, either the test is too difficult or the class has not mastered the subject. An examination of this special kind, in which most of the class obtains over 75% marks, is a bad examination ; it tells the teacher too little, for it does not really test the class.

In this type of examination the allocation of marks to individual answers must, of course, be made with the desired end in view. The teacher who generously spills high marks over merely creditable attempts in composition, for example, only deceives himself and the class. An experienced

examiner says that the golden rule for those
who mark papers is to be fairly liberal up to the pass
mark standard and niggardly in the higher reaches.
This hardly applies to answers in which there is
no question of absolute right and wrong, as there
would be in simple " mechanical " sums, or in
spellings or declensions, but to answers without
glaring errors which are to be judged for their
adequacy and fullness. The counsel is entirely
inapplicable to short tests given in the course of
teaching ; if the answers to a set of problems in
mental arithmetic are wrong, they are wrong and
there is an end of it.

In interpreting the results of a " full-dress "
examination the nature of the test must be borne
in mind. If the class is to be strung out of set
purpose the criterion of the success of the class
is how they are strung out—where the " peak "
in a graph comes. If the pass mark is 40% and
the paper is rightly set and properly marked, a
teacher may be satisfied if the " peak " is beyond
40%. The numbers who gain less than 40%, and
the steepness of graduations of the curve up to the
peak will inform him of the condition of his
weaker pupils, as will the curve on the other side
of 40% tell him what kind of top he has. For
estimating the success of a class a graph is more
useful than an average, for averages are liable to
be disturbed by special conditions, and they cannot
be relied upon unless numbers are large.

Although examinations do not always conform
exactly and clearly to either of the types discussed,

the distinction is worth keeping in mind. Many teachers in the past have treated their weekly (or even daily) tests as if they were tests for promotion, and as if the only end of teaching was to enable a class to do well at the terminal review. Thus dictation has been misused. It is a teaching method and is valuable as such, but when the dictation is of precisely the same kind as should occur in a terminal examination its value is greatly diminished. Here, as in all examinations, the main principle is to consider the purpose of the test and to model it accordingly.

We cannot assent to the opinion of some writers on education that examinations are an unmitigated evil under all conditions. If children are led to think of them as a kind of bogey, as a painful struggle with a mysterious and elusive opponent who is likely to be victorious in spite of all effort, then examinations are really harmful. If the object of the test is clearly understood, and yet such a fuss is made of it that the children are over-strained and nervously excited, the effect is bad, not only at the moment but during preparation. A temporary strain may soon be over, but if cramming takes the place of methodical learning, the evil results last longer.

All this can be allowed without abandoning the practice of examination altogether. For, as things now are, it is part of the ordinary machinery of instruction, in classes and schools, necessary as a convenient mode of reviewing the work done by the pupils before the next step in learning is begun.

Moreover, although the finer results of education cannot be tested by a formal examination, the acquisition of positive knowledge, and the ability to apply it in familiar and in novel situations, can be so tested. Even the mature student, educating himself alone with a deliberate purpose, must, from time to time, take stock of what he has learnt, and in some sense examine himself as part of the process of learning. So examinations, conducted in a matter-of-fact manner, must be looked upon as part of the ordinary programme.

If examinations are not to be injurious or wasteful of time, the right occasions and the purposes they serve on each occasion must be clearly understood by both teacher and pupil. They are periodical reviews. As such they must not come too often on a comprehensive scale. The frequent testing in arithmetic or rapid recall of spellings or points in grammar need not count as examinations, for they are part of the method of teaching.

External examinations are an undoubted bugbear, unless they are in harmony with the whole work of the school. At present they seem to be necessary, though many controversies arise as to their scope and suitability. All the young teacher can do is to guard against interpreting their results in a false perspective. Neither external nor internal examinations can be used as giving a final verdict upon a child's ability. Nor does success or failure in after life always follow upon success or failure in examinations. These commonplaces are mentioned only to remind the young teacher to keep a sober attitude towards examinations, with a just estimate of their value for the immediate purposes of his teaching, but without undue anxiety as to their ultimate importance for the future of those who are examined.

Some nonsense has also been talked about the dangers of the competitive spirit in schools. If it permeates the whole of the work of a class, so that learning becomes a mere race for marks, then competition is manifestly wrong, because it deflects teacher and pupils from the ends they should be pursuing. But no great harm can result from the good-humoured rivalry of a healthy set of boys and girls in an examination. The nervous child, who takes the struggle too seriously, must be placed *hors concours*. The chief competitor of a particular pupil should be himself, and the idea of beating his own record should be sedulously cultivated. This is a real preparation for life, for the desire to improve upon one's own performances is a constant and salutary stimulus.

M

CHAPTER XIV

INSTRUCTION AND EDUCATION

In the greater part of this book we have been discussing teaching as a craft. The young teacher has been urged to make himself a competent craftsman, and, while not forgetting ideals, to busy himself with the technique of his profession. He has been reminded from time to time that to aim at skill in craftsmanship has nothing of the ignoble in it, and that the very multiplicity and variety of the problems put before him must raise the true craft of teaching far above the commonplace. Yet the business of teaching is something more than craftsmanship, and something different from it. Craftsmanship appears to be concerned principally with instruction : teaching in its best sense should mean education. How far should the young teacher limit himself to instruction ? Is he not also to educate ?

The antithesis between instruction and education cannot be fully worked out here. Broadly speaking, and as commonly understood, instruction seems to imply that with the help of the teacher the pupil acquires a certain body of knowledge which he must possess in order to live a useful life in the community. Education goes beyond the acquisition of knowledge, and means a training in right habits and right thought, and these, in their turn, should blossom into right conduct and good character. It would be generally held that though the conveying of instruction may admit of a technique, the training towards right conduct and good character is an undertaking too subtle to be subject to the rules of a technique. One can advise and demonstrate how a piece of craftsmanship can be executed ; but the human personalities which have to be influenced are not like the material upon which a craftsman works, and not even like the orderly mass of knowledge upon which the teacher and pupil are employed.

All this is doubtless true, and in this book there is no attempt to sketch a technique in education. But the antithesis must not be pressed too far, and no discouraging corollaries should be drawn. If the children of this country were thoroughly well grounded in necessary knowledge, well instructed only, it would be a great achievement. The possession of knowledge, it is true, does not ensure the right use of it, any more than the possession of bodily fitness and strength means that these will be invariably employed for proper purposes. But one cannot pass through the training which results in sound knowledge or in physical fitness without acquiring on the way some healthy interests, or, at the lowest, without being introduced to some such interests, and healthy interests are one of the surest guarantees against the misapplication of powers.

Further, " mere instruction," as it is slightingly termed, if systematically carried on, has certain effects which can fairly be reckoned as contributions towards the training of character. The purport of what has been said in the preceding pages will have been strangely misconceived if it is not evident that teaching, as it is understood in this book, is a co-operative effort in which both partners work alike,—those who learn and those who teach. The co-operation which we have sketched entails a training in certain good habits and the cultivation of certain good qualities. It can be accomplished only by steady fostering of honesty, punctuality and perseverance ; it should stimulate and satisfy a spirit of inquiry, and it calls for self reliance and a willingness to face difficulties, including necessary drudgery. It should cultivate a promptness of response on all occasions, a habit of self control, of which the fruits are accuracy and exactitude, tidiness and carefulness, all manifested in a measure appropriate to the child's age. These qualities cannot fail to be produced in some degree by the good craftsmanship which should be the immediate aim of the young teacher. In so far as they are established in a pupil, they form a solid basis of good character.

The habits and qualities thus described do not, alone and in themselves, constitute a good character. They are rather habits and qualities which make for efficiency in any sphere of action. They do not

in themselves guide the pupil towards the right
kind of action, still less do they furnish him with
lofty ideals of conduct. For the higher elements
of character other influences than those which are
included under skilful instruction must be brought
to bear. Some of these influences are conveyed
by the whole school of which the young teacher's
class forms a part, by the *ethos*, the atmosphere and
tone, of the school. Such are the recognition of
lawful authority and loyal obedience to it, with
corporate feeling and spirit, a readiness to submerge
the individual and his desires and interests in
favour of the community, good sportsmanship and
fair play, a standard of decent behaviour in and
out of school.

Now although the school as a whole is rightly
regarded as something above the classes that it
contains, an entity to which allegiance is owed,
apart from the allegiance owing to the class, it
must not be forgotten that a good school means
good classes within it, and that the qualities of
character which mark it must be manifested in their
own degree in the individual classes. As the teacher
of one of these classes, the veriest beginner must
be contributing in some way, however modest, to
the *ethos* of the school. He cannot help himself.
Being a person in authority in contact with other
persons under him, he exerts a powerful influence,
and although his attention may be concentrated
upon the technique of teaching he is all the time
educating as well as instructing. He is training
character by the standard he sets, by his expectation

that his pupils will do their best, by his manifest impatience with work that is scamped, and by the example of his own attitude, not only in general towards his own work, but on particular occasions when a moral judgment must be given.

There are no counsels of " method " for this aspect of teaching, no " technique " of exerting a right personal influence. The young teacher will have to rely upon his own uprightness and common sense, and trust to his intuition in an emergency. But in a case of difficulty he had better consult, not books, but someone older and more experienced, to whom the whole story may be told. He should not worry about his responsibility in an over-conscientious way ; the faithful performance of that part of his duty where his course is clear, aided by his own sense of what is right, will make of him a good educator as well as a good teacher.

Finally, beyond the qualities so far sketched there lie even loftier constituents of good character ; reverence, a perception of beauty and of goodness, with a sense of ultimate realities culminating in religion. These also lie outside the art of teaching considered as craftsmanship. But they do not lie outside the teacher's duty.

The tradition of the school, exemplified in its past and active in the present, should inculcate and suggest something beyond the mere school decencies and proprieties. The right choice of what is worth teaching, especially in literature, will contribute much. The judicious head of a school will use occasions of public solemnity to give utterance, from time to time, to what will ordinarily remain unspoken. But for the most part the individual teacher will not consciously and of set purpose turn high ideals and lofty conceptions into subjects of homily.

CHAPTER XV

It would be well if all teachers kept constantly in mind the saying that " Nobody is ever competently wise save by his own wisdom." It is not enough to present knowledge to the young. Nor is it enough to present it in a workmanlike fashion, arranged and illustrated in accordance with their years. We must somehow contrive to ensure that the knowledge we present is assimilated, that it becomes a permanent part of the mental texture of the pupil, affecting his thought and action throughout, and being always available for some real purpose. Knowledge thus acquired is material for instruction in the true sense, for it is built into the fabric of the mind.

This building-in demands such frequent repetition of essential facts and processes as will ensure their ready and certain use when needed. It also demands that this use shall be practised in ways and on tasks which are appropriate to the stage reached by the pupil. The homely proverb, " It is by smiting that one becomes a smith," finds its echo in the teaching maxim, " Learn by doing," and in the many devices for promoting individual work and self-activity which are now advocated. Such devices have their general justification in the well-known fact that children are active rather than passive. They prefer to be doing something or making something instead of sitting still to hear discourses, although when their appetite for movement is temporarily satisfied they will listen readily enough to the right kind of oral lesson. School, however, is not merely a place of activity for children with provision for entertaining them when they are tired. It must be a place of disciplined activity, offering pursuits, experiences and lessons which will gradually develop in the pupils a body of practical and theoretical knowledge which they have learned to apply with intelligence and self-control. The young teacher should aim at giving to his pupils the fullest possible opportunity for learning things in a practical way, but he should not adopt uncritically any " method " or " system." The principle is what matters most, and no teaching device, however ingenious, can be made to apply universally and in all circumstances.

Thus it is unnecessary to carry the principle of self-activity to the point of requiring that the child shall re-discover everything for himself. The " heuristic " or " finding out " method can be used with profit to illustrate the ways by which knowledge is gained and verified. It should not be used in the vain hope of enabling a child to retraverse, in a few years of schooling, the long road by which the human mind has reached its present attainment of knowledge and power. Nor should the teacher accept the crude notion that children must not use scientific or technical terms. Apart from the fact that children are only too ready to use big words, there is no advantage in encouraging them to speak of " chalk-stuff gas " when they should be thinking of carbon di-oxide. In general, the teacher should examine all devices with a critical eye, especially such as offer a systematic scheme for the ordering of childish experiences and activities. Children imbibe knowledge and acquire aptitudes through many channels, and over-systematisation of a few may result in a closing of the others.

The natural activity of children is a valuable asset to the teacher, but its value depends upon right use. For example, we know that children are fond of making things, but this does not justify us in devising a sequence of dull exercises in the use of tools. Such exercises are the outcome of analysis by adult minds and they have no appeal for children. A child will undertake any amount of drudgery where it is clearly in line with his purpose, but drudgery in itself and for a purpose which is hidden from him will induce a dislike of all learning. Ask him to make a dovetail joint as a thing in itself, part of a sequence of exercises in handwork, and he will bring to the task little innate enthusiasm. But ask him to make such a joint as a necessary part of the butterfly cabinet which he wants to make and he will practise the exercise with zest, unmindful of its difficulty, and resolved to attain perfection.

The principle thus illustrated should be applied in all forms of activity in teaching. Sometimes the ultimate purpose cannot be understood by the child, as, for example, learning multiplication tables, formulæ, dates in history, or declensions in grammar. Here we may substitute an intermediate purpose, but it must be in line with the ultimate one. Rewards and marks may be used to stimulate effort, but every possible means should be devised for applying the knowledge or facility gained by the children. We can invent exercises for the purpose, and these will serve to show that the drudgery is not entirely meaningless. The practice of scales on the piano is tedious if it is never relieved by attempts to play a tune, and the attempt to play a tune which has been properly chosen for the purpose may demonstrate to the pupil the need for practising finger exercises. In varying measure every school subject affords occasion for practical work on the part of the pupil. In arithmetic and early mathematics there is much to be gained from measurement and the construction of shapes and figures. In reading we have voice exercises and oral work. In geography models and maps may be made, and in history we may have charts, maps, lines of time and illustrative diagrams. It is well to encourage children to express their ideas in diagrams, and this is a different thing from giving them diagrams to be copied. Such independent diagrams are not to be expected from young pupils, but the seniors should make them wherever possible.

We may now consider briefly some of the common-est forms of active learning, noting, however, that some kind of physical activity on the part of the pupil is a valuable aid in all school work. There are subjects in which it is more prominent than in others, being indeed indispensable. Thus a child cannot learn to write, to sing, to make things or to play games without some physical effort on his own part. In such learning he must gain proficiency by repeated practice, and the teacher's part is to ensure that the practice is well-ordered for the end in view. It must be economical of time and of labour, seasoned with interest, and directed to the formation of appropriate habits of move-ment. Such habits are the outcome of exercises, carefully and accurately repeated until the move-ments, or relative positions of nerve and muscle, are accomplished as needed and with a minimum of conscious direction. Skill in any form of bodily activity contains a large element of automatic motion, the result of repeated practice. It needs no great amount of reflection to enable us to see that changes in the practice will tend to delay the formation of the habit. If we are making a track across a snow-covered field we shall attain success most quickly if we go over the same route again and again, instead of making a fresh path each time. Every diversion from the first route will delay the completion of the track. This illustration carries the further lesson that we should choose our route in the first instance with the greatest care, so as to avoid waste of time and effort.

Clearly, too, we should know the point which we desire to reach. The foregoing principles are exemplified in the following notes on familiar school activities.

Handwriting.

Here we are aiming to secure legibility, speed, and beauty of form. Writing is a special kind of drawing, very difficult for young children by reason of the instrument and materials employed. A child has not developed the co-ordination of nerve and muscle which is required to govern small movements and to perform delicate operations with pen or pencil. Yet he can gain a lasting mental impression of the shapes of letters by making big movements with arm and hand. He may begin by making the shapes in the air or by drawing them in coloured chalks on sheets of brown paper or on blackboards. This process of gaining a mental impression of letter shapes is helped by the old device of sand-trays in which the letters can be traced and erased very easily. Another device, which can be turned into a game, is that of having the letters cut out in fine glasspaper, mounted on cards. The cards are distributed face downwards and the children close their eyes before turning their cards over and trying to identify the letters by touch.

At this stage it is obviously convenient to practise the shapes which the child is seeing constantly in his reading book, and hence we find in many schools of to-day that the first lessons in writing are in what is called print-script, as distinct from the old copperplate longhand. This method of beginning to write has the sanction of history, since the earliest printed letters were based on the current script of the time. But although it is useful as a foundation the print-script must not be retained beyond reason. The history of penmanship shows how formal script always develops into a cursive or running hand as the need for greater speed is felt. Hence the teacher should be ready to suggest forms of letters and of joining which will not impair the legibility of the script first learned, nor involve the breaking of a new path, but will aid in developing speed. It should be noted that legibility and speed are aided by strict conformity in the shapes of the letters and by treating words as units. Correct spacing, with intervals of white between the words, will help the reader.

Handwriting is a matter of practice, and it is worth while to have a few words, a sentence, or a paragraph, written out slowly and carefully every day. The craft of penmanship will attract some of the pupils, and all should be encouraged to study good examples. Printed reproductions of portions of old manuscripts are to be obtained from the British Museum and elsewhere. Beginning with a somewhat laboured drawing of enlarged letter shapes the pupils may pass gradually through exercises in smaller forms until they can write clearly and fairly rapidly in a script which is ready to merge into a seemly and readable running hand. These lessons should be marked by a constant insistence on neat and tidy work and the children should be led to take pride in producing a handwriting which has claims to beauty. The teacher will find that the handwriting of his class seems to go to pieces when they are introduced to a fresh application of writing. The boy who writes well in transcription will write badly when he begins dictation, or still more badly if he writes an essay. The reason is that the movements for handwriting are not yet automatic, and they become ill-directed when the attention is diverted to spelling words or making sentences. The remedy is to maintain the practice, already suggested, of having a little daily drill in formal writing.

Drawing.

Properly speaking, drawing should be considered before handwriting, and a child should be allowed to draw long before he is required to write. Early and even desultory practice with chalk or coloured crayons on large surfaces affords excellent physical activity. At school the teacher should be careful to avoid over-direction. The old method of treating drawing as a series of ordered exercises beginning with straight lines and ending with a perspective representation of a hexagonal prism is happily discredited. The modern view wisely limits the responsibility of the teacher to the effort to release artistic aptitude in his pupils by showing them how to use pencil, crayon, or paint in the manner most likely to enable them to convey their impressions to paper or canvas. He will show them how the materials are used, but he will not try to make them see things as he sees them, still less to make them content with conventional representations alone. He will give hints on the composition of a picture, and illustrate them by well-chosen examples of great works, but he will not prescribe anything. His task is to encourage adventure in drawing and in painting, reserving his teaching until it becomes worth while. He will then be at pains to discover what the pupil was trying to do, and by judicious counsel and criticism he will encourage and help him in a fresh effort. Apart from formal lessons in drawing the school itself should foster artistic perception. Rooms should be well-proportioned, and each should contain some object or picture of artistic merit. It is unwise to multiply such things, however, and it is wise to arrange for exchanges between different rooms to guard against that over-familiarity which prevents us from seeing things. More use should be made of colour in school decoration, and if the young teacher should find himself condemned to work in a room with the all too common liver-coloured dado and bathroom green walls he should protect his pupils and himself by hanging a few prints in bold colours or by arranging a decorative frieze to distract the eye.

Music.

Singing is a natural activity in childhood, and this is now recognised in most schools. Every teacher should be able to lead a class in " community singing," choosing a repertory of suitable songs.

This demands no great knowledge of music, no more at any rate than should be possessed by anybody who lives with children for several hours of each day. There will be formal lessons in music, and possibly some children may be learning the pianoforte or another instrument. Such instruction is a matter for the specialist, but he will do well to remember that it is fatally easy to destroy musical interest in children by compelling them to approach the art along adult-made paths. Singing is the best approach for children, but they must be taught to use their voices properly and without strain. Here the advice of the musician may be helpful, but it is always a safe rule to insist on quiet rather than loud singing. Beginning with simple melodies, it becomes possible to use these later as a means of learning the language of written music, the children learning to interpret the signs used in writing the songs they can already sing. Tonic Sol-fa is an aid, but ability to read music in this notation is not enough, since all Western music is written in the staff notation, and ability to read it is essential to all who sing or play an instrument.

The young teacher should exercise great care in the choice of songs. They should be well within the range of the children's voices, and well-suited to their years. Fortunately there are now available many collections of old English melodies and many charming songs by modern composers. A class might learn three or more songs a term, and there could be no pleasanter way of spending five minutes before playtime or between two lessons than in

N

singing one or two songs. The practice would foster a liking for real music and furnish an antidote to cheap and shoddy airs which often become popular outside school.

Handwork.

Of handwork in general little need be said. The young teacher who is concerned with this branch of work will probably have taken a special course of training. It is worth noting, however, that such activities as woodwork and metalwork are not undertaken in order to make carpenters or mechanics. They are in fact somewhat tardy and imperfectly developed attempts to give assent to the view that " most children think with their hands rather than with their brains." The view is correct, and it has been established beyond doubt, but we have not yet applied it fully in the schools. When we do apply it we shall use handwork as a medium of instruction in many subjects, treating technique or skill in manual operations as a means to an end rather than an end in itself. From the beginning it is desirable to cultivate deftness of hand by practising manipulation in paper, cardboard, and other simple materials. At each stage the skill thus gained should be applied to the making of things such as children desire to make. This kind of teaching has the great merit of enabling the pupil to judge his own work. Opinion as to the merit of an essay or other written exercise may vary, and it is often difficult to make the pupil see the reason for an adverse judgment. But there can be no argument as to whether a piece of handwork is successfully accomplished. Merit and fault are alike plainly visible, and it is easy to compare two attempts at making the same thing. Handwork has the further and most valuable attribute of giving scope to pupils who do not respond readily to verbal or literary instruction. Such children are often discouraged by finding themselves regarded as dull or stupid according to ordinary school standards. Given the opportunity, they will often excel in handwork, and thereby recover or maintain that self-respect which should never be destroyed in youth.

Other Activities.

On the sound principle that every pupil in a school should be regarded as an active member of the community, the young teacher will encourage the formation of a class collection of things of interest. Such a collection should not be allowed to become a mere dry museum. It should be kept in free circulation, as it were, the objects being reviewed frequently, some being discarded and others, it may be, passing on to the general school museum. Children like to show to others the things which interest themselves, and occasional special exhibits of toys, home-made especially, of collections of stamps, butterflies, fossils or plants, will suggest activities and pursuits to those who need the stimulus. The museum should be a living thing, and not merely a collection of curiosities to excite a passing wonder.

CHAPTER XVI

Books to Consult : Some Suggestions

In the present chapter we offer a list of books for the young teacher to consult. The notes that accompany the list are intended to guide him in his choice. Some of the books are suggested because they contain practical details which could not be included in our previous chapters ; for example, on special methods of teaching. There are also systematic treatises on subjects like psychology, or the philosophical bases of education, on which we can barely touch. Others again are manuals which cover much the same ground as the present work, but are on a scale more comprehensive than has been here possible. The order in which the books are presented is by no means the order in which they should necessarily be read. The young teacher is advised to read first that which attracts him most or that which he needs first to supplement what we have been able to supply. It is desirable that all teachers should study aspects of education beyond those which concern them in their day to day work in the class-room. But the study is so wide and ramifies in so many directions, into philosophy, sociology, history, biology, that very few can hope to survey the whole ground. The young teacher is advised to pursue the line of his own interest. He may be attracted by the history of education, and wish to trace out for his own satisfaction the development of the great educational ideas which have governed the world and their interrelation with the growth of thought. He may be interested more in persons than in ideas, and find a delight in the biographies of great teachers. Psychology, especially in its modern forms, has a fascination for many teachers. Some of them also may like to explore the relations between the development of children and that of other forms of young life. Others are at home in the region of philosophy ; they will find material in plenty for speculation and even for controversy. Again the organisation of education may appeal to some who will compare system with system in different countries and ages. Very many, perhaps, overwhelmed by their daily work, will have little leisure for study very far removed from their ordinary pursuits but will be keenly alert on the practical side, and anxious to study the niceties of method or the social activities of schools. The important thing is that no one should rust or grow stale, and that each should have a mind with a growing point.

A. *General Principles of Education.*

The following books discuss from different points of view the general principles of education. They all contain chapters upon the application of the principles to the living problems of the schools. In each there are references to books which deal more fully with specific questions.

All of these relate to English conditions:

Education, its Data and First Principles. T. P. Nunn (Arnold, 1920).

The Foundations of Education: 2 vols. J. J. Findlay (University of London Press, 1926, 1927).

The Nation's Schools. H. Bompas Smith (Longmans, 1927).

The books of Professor Campagnac—*Society and Solitude* (Cambridge University Press) ; *Converging Paths* (Cambridge University Press); *Education in Relation to the Common Purposes of Humanity* (Pitman)—also deal with principles though in a less systematic way.

B. *Psychology.*

As an introduction to psychology, and in order to become familiar with the outlines, the student is advised to begin with the following books :

Talks to Teachers on Psychology and Life's Ideals. Wm. James (Longmans).

Psychology. Wm. MacDougall (Home University Library).

Herbartian Psychology. John Adams (Longmans).

Introduction to Psychology. Loveday and Green (Oxford University Press).

After these, the student has a wide choice. Besides the large treatises on psychology as a science (e.g. by Wm. James, Stout, etc.), there are books which bear more or less directly on education. Such are :

Psychology Applied to Education. James Ward (Cambridge University Press).

Social Psychology. Wm. MacDougall (Methuen).

Psychology for Teachers. Lloyd Morgan (Arnold).

The Educative Process. W. G. Bagley (Macmillan).

Instinct, Intelligence and Character. Godfrey Thomson (Allen and Unwin).

Educational Psychology. Chas. Fox (Kegan Paul).

Besides these there are books designed as students' manuals by Professor Drever, B. Dumville, Mrs. S. Brierley and others. More specific in scope are two books on character :

The Making of Character. J. MacCunn (Cambridge University Press).

The Dawn of Character. Edith A. Mumford (Longmans).

The student interested in Experimental Psychology might begin with *An Introduction to Experimental Psychology*, by C. S. Myers (Cambridge University

Press, 1914), or *Introduction to Experimental Psychology* by C. W. Valentine (University Tutorial Press). For information on Intelligence Tests the student should consult in the first instance the Report of the Consultative Committee of the Board of Education on *Psychological Tests of Educable Capacity* (H.M. Stationery Office) and follow up the reading this will suggest.

C.   *Methods of Teaching.*

We have already referred in Chapter VIII to the " Suggestions " of the Board of Education.   The full title is—

> *Handbook of Suggestions for the Consideration of Teachers and Others concerned in the Work of Public Elementary Schools* (H.M. Stationery Office. 2s. net).

The book contains chapters on all the subjects (except religious instruction) ordinarily taught in elementary, including central, schools.   The range of age is up to fifteen years.   Languages other than English are omitted ; it may be noted that the teaching of Welsh was the subject of investigation by a special committee which has issued an interesting report.   Except for languages, and special subjects such as those associated with commerce, the ground covered by the Suggestions is the same as that covered in all schools which teach children up to fifteen.   The Suggestions, therefore, are of value to teachers in Preparatory and other Independent Schools, as well as, with appropriate modifications, to teachers of small groups of children or individual pupils. As we stated before, the book is one of suggestions only, which, as the prefatory note points out, are to be " regarded as a challenge to independent thought on the subjects treated."

Several useful manuals have been written for the use of students in training. These usually contain, not only chapters on principles of teaching and on the general rules of method, but specific directions in detail on particular modes of handling each subject.

Principles of Education. T. Raymont (Longmans).

Principles and Methods of Teaching. J. Welton (University Tutorial Press).

Principles of Class Teaching. J. J. Findlay (Macmillan).

The Practice of Instruction. J. W. Adamson (National Society).

The two books which follow were written mainly with secondary schools in view ; they were first published in 1897 and 1899 :

Teaching and Organisation. P. A. Barnett (Longmans).

Common Sense in Education and Teaching. P. A. Barnett (Longmans).

Useful books on present-day ideas and practice in teaching are :

The New Teaching. Edited by John Adams (Hodder and Stoughton).

Educational Movements and Methods. Edited by John Adams (Harrap).

The Board of Education has from time to time published pamphlets on the teaching of subjects in Secondary Schools. They have not been gathered into a Handbook, for they are rather for specialist teachers. The Scottish Education Department has a similar series. Of decided general interest, not only to teachers but to the public, are longer Reports on the position of English, Modern Languages, Science and Classics in the Educational System of Great Britain. All these are procurable from H.M. Stationery Office. The Report on English concerns all teachers.

Some useful suggestions on the curriculum and methods appropriate for post-primary schools are to be found in the Report of the Consultative Committee (1926)—*The Education of the Adolescent.*

Certain present day experiments in methods of teaching, to which occasional allusion has been made in the previous chapters, are best studied in the special books which advocate them. Some of them, however, are discussed in *Educational Movements and Methods* above mentioned and in the same editor's *Modern Developments in Educational Practice* (University of London Press). We can quote only a few of these special books :

The Play Way. H. Caldwell Cook (1917, Heinemann).

The Montessori Method ; translated from the Italian (Heinemann).

The Montessori Manual. D. C. Fisher (Constable).

Education on the Dalton Plan. Helen Parkhurst (Bell).

Towards Freedom—the Howard Plan. Dr. O'Brien Harris (University of London Press).

An Essay towards a Philosophy of Education. Charlotte M. Mason (Kegan Paul).

Miss Mason was the originator of the method of the P.N.E.U. (Parents National Educational Union), and this body has issued a number of books bearing upon the method. Governesses and private tutors would do well to make themselves familiar with these publications.

There is not space to include the numerous books which are written upon the teaching of particular subjects, and it is somewhat invidious to make selections.

D. *The Teaching of Young Children.*

The Dawn of Mind. M. Drummond (Arnold).

Education by Life. H. Brown-Smith (H. Phillips).

Five Years Old or Thereabouts. M. Drummond (Arnold).

The Child; its Nature and Nurture. W. B. Drummond (Dent).

The Child under Eight. E. B. Murray and H. B. Smith (Arnold).

Handwork and its Place in Early Education. L. L. Plaisted (Oxford University Press).

The Art of Story-telling. Marie L. Shedlock (1915. Murray).

Education by Plays and Games. G. E. Johnson (Ginn and Co.).

Speech Defects. I. C. Ward (Dent).

The Montessori books mentioned under C bear especially upon the education of young children.

E. *History of Education.*

The following are perhaps the most suitable books to begin upon. They will suggest further reading :

A Short History of Education. J. W. Adamson (1919. Cambridge University Press).

A Survey of the History of Education. Helen Wodehouse (1925. Arnold).

Secondary Education in the XIXth Century. R. L. Archer (1922. Cambridge University Press).

The Great Educators Series (Heinemann).

F. *Health and Physical Training.*

This topic should be considered in the light of the comprehensive work of Dr. James Kerr (*Fundamentals of School Health*, George Allen and Unwin). This book is expensive, but it may be seen in libraries, while for text book purposes there are available many smaller books such as *School Hygiene.* Lyster (University Tutorial Press).

The best handbooks on Physical Training are those issued by the Board of Education through H.M. Stationery Office.

INDEX